FINDING KATHERINE

Finding Katherine: A Spiritual Journey to Vietnam and Motherhood
by Ellen Fitzenrider

Published by Mindful Media
914 Gates Avenue, Norfolk, VA 23517
www.mindfulmediabooks.com

Cover and Interior Book Design by Pneuma Books, LLC
For more info, visit www. pneumabooks.com

Cover art: *Katherine*, 2003. Artist: Gail O'Neill
www.impressionedview.com

Printed in the United States on acid-free paper by Thomson-Shore, Dexter, Michigan. www.tshore.com

09 08 07 06 05   6 5 4 3 2 1

Publisher's Cataloging-In-Publication Data
(*Prepared by the Donohue Group, Inc.*)

Fitzenrider, Ellen.
    Finding Katherine : a spiritual journey to Vietnam and motherhood / Ellen Fitzenrider. -- 2nd ed. --

        p. : ill. ; cm.
    Includes resource page listing organizations dealing with international adoption.
        ISBN: 0-9745694-3-7
        LCCN: 2003112620

1. Adoption. 2. Intercountry adoption. 3. Mothers and daughters. 4. Spiritual life--Buddhism. 5. Vietnam--Social life and customs. I. Title.

HV875.5 .F58 2004
362.734

FINDING KATHERINE

A Spiritual Journey to Vietnam and Motherhood

Dr. Ellen Fitzenrider

Dedicated to La Thi Huong, my daughter, Katherine,
without whom this adventure never would have happened.
…and to Quay.

Acknowledgements

I would like to thank my friends and family for being supportive throughout the process of writing and editing and editing and editing this story. Special thanks to Donna Rienzo who spent so many hours with me refining how it was all said. To Judith Mosely, who helped me to find Katherine. To my step-mom, Betty, who shared the chapters of all revisions with her entire neighborhood for input. For my mom, who helped with editing right down to the wire. To the APV list members, who made so much of this journey possible, and who continue to be a support. To the Lunar Landing Café for allowing me a little table in the corner for countless hours. To my *sangha* members, the Mindfulness Community of Hampton Roads, and Allen Sandler, for inspiration. To the People of Vietnam, for sharing some of their beauty with me. To Gail O'Neill, whose wonderful artwork captures the essence of my daughter. To Tuyen Nguyen for Vietnamese translation, language assistance and friendship.

I hope that this work properly honors all of you.

~ Metta

Table of Contents

List of Photographs

FINDING
KATHERINE

Introduction

MY 38TH BIRTHDAY found me sitting outside of my favorite coffee-house taking stock of my dreams and fears. I was a once-married, now single woman. I was a successful professional who had managed to fill my life with rewarding work and a diverse group of friends. I loved where I lived and I had taken advantage of opportunities to travel and experience cultures in many forms. I had many blessings in my life, and could even honestly say that I had achieved what I found to be the most elusive of states: a sense of peace.

Yet there was one sorrow that would cast its shadow over my life from time to time. It was the unfulfilled expectation that I had brought along the journey of my life since childhood. I wanted to be a mommy. If you had asked me to list fifty, or even just ten concrete reasons why it was so important to me, I might have been hard-pressed. Deep down, the feeling in my gut, in my heart, was that I couldn't even fully imagine what motherhood would be without having experienced it. But I knew, perhaps intuitively, that I had to make it a part of my journey in this lifetime.

I was 38 years old, however. As much as I hated to admit it, the proverbial biological clock was ticking, and there was no 'significant other' in my life. At least not with whom I wanted to

1

share the rest of my life, let alone parenthood. And I refused to settle for "Mr. Wrong" just to become a mommy.

The concept of adoption wasn't a part of my direct family experience, but I held no prejudices against it. I gave it some more thought, which brought me to confronting a new set of fears: Would I be able to handle life as a single parent? Could I do this all by myself? How do I know that I would fall in love with this child? How do I know that she will fall in love with me?

With these fears in my mind but my vision clearly in front of me like a beacon, I decided to take the first step on a new, unfamiliar journey...

Chapter 1

GRAY, MIST-SHROUDED MOUNTAINS gradually lengthen and stretch and flatten out, like a cat laying itself out in the sun, relaxing and opening. Silent peaks transform into the structured squares and rectangles of rice paddies, shimmering with brilliant green and the sparkle of water. What was dark and mysterious, secretive even, has become vibrant and colorful and full of life. "It is not permissible to take photographs from the airplane." The human voice over the intercom contrasts vividly with the raw scene of nature below us.

I continue to rest my cheek on the smooth plastic covering the window, my eyes taking the pictures that I will keep with me forever. I have spent the past 24 hours in the air, transferring three times: in Chicago, Seoul and Hong Kong. I have come to meet my daughter. She doesn't know that I am coming yet. I sit and think about Lily, close my eyes and try to hone-in on her little body. In my mind's eye, I travel to a crib in a room in an orphanage in a city called Lang Son in the north of Vietnam. I have made this mental trip many times during the past four weeks while sitting on the couch in my living room in Norfolk, Virginia. In my wallet is a photo of a round-faced, one-year-old girl, with a pointed little chin and a serious expression on her face. It is a photo that I have fallen in love with and looked at many times a day, hungrily devouring the tiniest details. Her Vietnamese name is Ly Thi Thanh. We will share our lives together. She doesn't know that yet, either.

It is difficult to reconcile the vision before my eyes with the images in my mind. Fields stretch as far as I can see, with clusters of buildings gathered here and there. Roads teem with trucks and automobiles, and, as we get closer and closer to the ground, bicycles and motorbikes and water buffalo magically appear from specks of dust. Everyone and everything is moving purposefully in all directions in a delicately choreographed but frenetic dance.

In my mind, however, the images of Vietnam that have collected over three decades are explosions and violence, dirt-and-fear-smeared American GI faces playing cat-and-mouse games with vicious inhuman enemies. Bodies separated from their parts, the crying of children and the juice of death. Scenes from war movies where, thirty-plus years ago, 'we' were trying to save somebody from something. Up until these past few months, when I began plowing through a handful of books to fill the gap that was what I didn't know, the reality of Vietnam as a place has been a mystery to me.

The plane lands in Hanoi, and I carry my backpack down a long corridor and find a little space in the mass of people waiting to get through customs. I am suffering from jet-lag and lack of sleep, but I find myself surprisingly calm and relaxed. The immensity of this journey somehow hovers over me, floating above, rather than resting on my shoulders.

I wait and breathe and move a few inches forward when the line moves. Stop, wait, and take another deep breath. No rush, no hurry. Waiting in line is one of the best places to practice one's breathing, and one of the places where you need it the most. Breathe in, breathe out. I try to clear my mind of everything but paying focused attention to this simple act of taking air into my lungs and letting it compress out slowly. This is a part of my Buddhist practice.

At the customs counter, my passport and VISA are finally inspected, and I pass on through in under a minute. I am carrying

over $8,000 in U.S. cash and traveler's checks in my fanny pack.
$7,000 is for the lawyer's fees for the adoption, $1,000 for the first
bit of traveling expenses. I trust my ATM card to get me through
anything else over the next two months. Up ahead, I see that my
suitcase is already making its way around and around on the conveyor belt. It is sandwiched between large trunks, duffle bags,
boxes and bags, all smothered in silver-gray duct tape. I squeeze
through the other waiting bodies and lift it up.

On the other side of the exit doors, there is a throng of people
waiting to pick up their passengers. Scanning the crowd for a name
placard that reads "Fitzenrider," I finally spot it in the hands of a
young-looking Vietnamese man about my height. Well, I'm five-
five, and all the men look about my height. Too young to be Binh, a
lawyer, I think, but that's him, holding up my name. He is the man
who e-mailed me that picture just a month ago. *Today I am sending
you this photo of Baby Thanh,*" the e-mail had said. "*If you would
like to adopt her, please let me know.*" Would I? *Would I?*

I greet this person whom I have only known on the Internet,
and he leads me to a black SUV. His English is fairly good and
carefully pronounced, but with an accent, and his sentences are
missing a word here and there like a lost puzzle piece. As the
driver pulls out into traffic, Binh tells me that it will be about a
forty-five minute ride until we reach downtown Hanoi, so I settle back to watch the scenery.

Most of the traffic is motorbikes, though there are some smaller
cars. Along the side of the road, people are walking, riding bicycles
or leading water buffalo laden with cargo. There are the rice paddies, shallowly flooded squares of land with various heights of
long, slender leaves rising out of it, blades of grass bending slightly
in the breeze. There are also scattered, well-worn houses, some of
them with red clay-tiled roofs that remind me of Spain.

And there is honking. Drivers of cars and motorbikes alike use
their horns like some kind of bat-sonar system, constantly tapping

to signal their presence, or laying on them hard when they want someone to get out of their way, or when a bike or pedestrian scuttles crab-like across the highway. Through all this, everyone seems totally calm. No angry outbursts or raised fists. No tempers flaring. No road rage. This is just how things are done.

The radio plays as we drive towards the city, and Binh and the driver don't talk either. The music is mostly American, and I smile to myself as they both whistle under their breath to the tunes: "Rhythm of the Falling Rain," and "Top of the World" by the Carpenters. Curious…each time the station plays a song, they play the original, then follow it up with a drawn out muzak-y instrumental version of the same song.

Soon we begin to see more visible signs that we are reaching the outskirts of Hanoi. We turn off the paved highway, and for a little while we are on a red clay access road. But here it is even more congested. The traffic continues to thicken, and the drivers of the motorbikes now wear bandanas or cloths over their noses and faces because the exhaust fumes and the red dust from the road are so dense. The brew swirls in circles into the air and settles thickly everywhere. Along both sides of the road are stalls selling everything imaginable, from fruits and vegetables to bricks to scrap cardboard to banana trees to sacks of rice and spices. No one can see the pale skin and wide hazel eyes peering out, fascinated, through the tinted windows of the SUV.

THIS DAY IS A LAST LEG of one journey and a first leg of another. It is the last leg of months of gathering paperwork, of interviews and getting fingerprinted. Of certifications and notarizations and financial statements, documents, papers and forms. Filling them out, organizing them, sending them, receiving them, getting them stamped, authenticated, certified, poked, prodded and punched. The backpack beside me on the seat has not for a second left my sight since leaving home. It contains this 'dossier' of about sixty pages, and it represents the end of a life where I can't imagine that I am really going to be a mommy.

I look out the window at the earth and the sky, the dancing swirls of red dust, and the milling people trying to maneuver around each other. This is the first leg of a new journey. Yes, I tell myself, I really, really am. I'm really going to be a mommy.

THE DIRT ROAD gives way again to pavement, and we are in Hanoi, which consists mostly of buildings only a few stories high, wide streets and very few traffic signals. And lots and lots of motorbikes. Some with one or two passengers, occasionally three, and frequently a whole family of four or five riding: Father driving, mother in the rear with one child between them, one child in front of the father, and a little one up at the handlebars. Everyone is honking their horns. When there are traffic signals, red lights are run, greens anticipated prematurely, or they are often ignored completely. I expect to see so many accidents within my first hour of arriving in the city, but it isn't long before I can see that there are rules...Vietnamese rules...but they create a kind of order in the chaos.

Binh brings me to a hotel with the unromantic name of Army Guesthouse. The front desk receptionists wear *ao dais*, the traditional silk outfit for women consisting of a long mid-calf length tunic top with slits up both sides to the waist with a Mandarin-style collar over flowing pants. A large Sony flatscreen TV is tuned to a Vietnamese news channel, and in the center of the lobby stands a tinseled Christmas tree. Binh makes sure that I am checked in, then says he will be back tomorrow (Monday, I think? Yes, I guess that I lost a day in there) at 10:30 so we can get my paperwork authenticated by the Vietnamese government.

AT TWO O'CLOCK, I am sitting cross-legged on the bed in my room after a failed attempt at a nap. My rest will instead be the relaxing of my body, bringing my attention to the endless rise and ebb of my breathing that normally escapes my conscious awareness. It serves to center my being into this room, at this moment only. Forget the past stressful twenty-four hours of traveling. Forget my lists of things to bring and what I might have forgotten. For a few moments I succeed in this meditation, and a calming salve spreads fluidly through my veins. I touch this place of 'just-being' long enough to savor the taste of it before I feel it slipping away just as elusively.

As those moments fade, a thought has entered my mind. I am just days away from meeting Lily. Lily Thanh Ly Fitzenrider, following the tradition of many families who adopt children and keep their Vietnamese name as the child's middle name. The face that I have memorized hovers behind my closed eyelids. I can feel her breathing with me.

I finally rise and head to the bathroom, where I take the picture of her out of my fannypack and prop it against the mirror. I look at my reflection, remembering a morning in August when I was getting ready for the day. I had just started filing the paperwork to adopt a little girl. A little girl that I was going to name Katherine, as I had always wanted to do since Katharine Hepburn was an idol in my teenage years.

That morning as I sleepily used a blow dryer on my hair, I looked into my own hazel eyes looking back at me and distinctly heard in my head "Lily." It was not a question. Although I hadn't been thinking about anything in particular at the time, I knew that it was the name of my daughter halfway across the world. Lily? Why Lily? I've never *known* a Lily. It hasn't been in the *plan*, or ever crossed my mind. But somehow that warm little body so far away was Lily, my daughter in the greater scheme of things, in all but presence only.

If we are to be mother and daughter for the decades of our lives, bringing whatever those decades will, and whatever the relationship will be, the matter of a few months and a few thousand miles was only a technicality. She is my destiny and I hers. Our co-destiny will be together, intertwined. We will each be changed by the other, each of our paths forever altered in so many large and infinitesimal ways because of the other.

Many philosophies believe that our spirits choose the body that we are going to enter before we are born, specifically choosing our parents, or a life situation so that we experience certain things or learn certain lessons, or have the chance to overcome specific obstacles. If one believes that the spirit can leave the body freely at death, that it does not die with the body, then why could it not have the freedom to enter another one just as easily, not just once, but over and over again? More than one time around? So many of the eastern religions contain this as part of their belief system, a given, including Buddhism. They see death as purely a brief segue into the next beginning, hopefully as a little bit wiser spirit because of lessons properly learned. I confess that I feel comfortable with this as part of my own personal spiritual medley of faith.

But my daughter, Lily, is laying in a crib just a few hours from where I stand right now, whose spirit entered her body around a year ago, and she did so over half a year before it even occurred to me to go down this path. If we truly are in each other's destiny, then somehow she had some advance notice. If my own belief system is to work, that is. Otherwise this whole thing will be one big fat chance occurrence with nobody having any say in how it falls into place. I can't help but think and feel that there is less randomness than there appears to be in life.

I unpack a few items and organize them on the shelves. Lily's things I leave in the bag. I won't need them for awhile. I do a quick survey though. Diapers, baby wipes and diaper bag. Formula, bottles, clothes, baby bowl and spoon. Little stuffed bear and elephant. Pacifier. All alien trappings to my life up until this moment. It seems hard to believe that they will soon feel as much a part of my accessories as my car keys and checkbook.

My adventurous spirit won't let me sit still for long, and I tear out the map pages of Hanoi from my *Rough Guide to Vietnam*, a trick I picked up on my previous travels. First of all, because it's easier to carry than a whole book. You can fold the pages up and slip them into your pocket, and you're less likely to leave it somewhere (like on top of a public phone: Amalfi, Italy, 1999). The other reason is to try to blend in…at least it has been in the past. Nothing brands you as a tourist more than standing on the Left Bank with a guidebook in your hand, and a puzzled look on your face as you look around for the street sign for *Rue St. Germain*, while Madame Foulard's yorkie pees on your foot.

Blending in is *not* an option for me in Hanoi, however. At every moment I am as conspicuous as a red hen in a flock of crows. From the moment I step out the hotel door, the cyclo (pronounced 'sicklow') drivers pester me to give me a ride. A cyclo is giant tricycle with a seat in the front that is big enough to carry about 1½ people. After declining a ride, choosing instead to walk, and heading down the block, I attract many glances, some covert, others more open. None threatening, all curious. Until I hit the Opera house, an imposing remnant from the days when Vietnam was a French colony. From out of nowhere, vendors selling postcards and embroidered t-shirts swoop down on me, and I have to protest multiple times as well as walk away quickly in order to extricate myself.

A block away, I stop to glance at my torn-out map pages and try to decide on a destination. At least I don't have to worry about lunch, as I'm still stuffed from breakfast. Breakfast was an adventure in itself! Being such an international hub, the hotel at the Hong Kong airport where I spent last night's layover really covered the bases. They had an unbelievable buffet, with stations set up by culture: the Japanese area had soba noodles with various toppings including something brown and crispy-looking, which ended up being little dried crushed fish (I finally figured out what they were when I saw the tiny little dried eyeballs); the English table had eggs and sausages and baked beans and mushrooms and tomatoes; the American setup was more eggs, hash browns and cereals; the Europeans got cheeses, cold cuts, fruit and breads and rolls; the Indians had vegetarian and non-vegetarian curries, and *samosas*; and, finally, the Chinese section had spring and egg rolls, a soupy-looking rice dish called *congee*, and stir-fried veggies and noodles. I ended up getting a little of everything. Everything that didn't have eyeballs in it, that is.

I head south, trying to get the hang of crossing the street. I would like to try to cross at a light, but they are few and far between. I observe other pedestrians, trying to discern the 'trick,' but it looks to me as if the trick is to just walk out. Once you do, don't pause or stop or change direction...that only confuses the motorists. You trust them to swerve around you.

I get a chance to look at shops and people-watch...people-watch the people watching *me*. Shops are clustered based on what it is they sell. One whole block is televisions and audio equipment. The next is large household appliances like washing machines. The next is children's clothing. Motorbikes are pulled up and parked on the sidewalks perpendicular to the street, and I have to weave my way around and through them, occasionally hopping into the street at several impassable stretches.

Along the way there are people sitting on steps, little plastic stools, boxes or just squatting, and conversing, sharing café or tea, or cooking and eating soup. Little stoves are set up right there along the sidewalk, and it seems that anyone can walk up and sit down for a café or bowl of noodle soup, called *pho*. Children are running around, shrieking, laughing, being called after by their parents, and there is an overturned open-weave basket over two chickens, serving as a cage.

As I walk, young men on motorbikes call out, "Miss...Miss...you want a ride?" They pat the space behind them on the seat. Rough Guide tells me that this is an informal form of transportation, and about 10,000 *dong* (15,000 *dong* is equal to a dollar) can get you an easy ride to somewhere else in the city. A good way to earn a little extra cash in a country where the average wage is less than a dollar a day. No, I smile and shake my head.

I have chosen as my first destination two lakes and a park, instead of Notre Dame Cathedral or the mausoleum of Uncle Ho — Ho Chi Minh. I go through a lot of city to get there, perhaps a mile and a half, when I come upon Thien Quang Lake. The traffic swirls around the thin rim of grass, trees and stone path that winds around the lake. Such a visual contrast to the noise of the motorbike engines, constantly beeping horns, and especially the trucks that have retrofitted their regular horns with air-horns and use them without mercy. It all creates a cacophonous bedlam.

At the edge of the water, there are people using hand held nets to scoop up little silver fish that swim near the surface, transferring them to buckets a few at a time. I eye the water suspiciously, imagining it to be less than pristine. A little further down, I see a man squatting down at the edge, facing away from the water, shirttails flapping in the breeze, defecating into the lake. What a dichotomy of beauty and, and—I'm a little speechless. I hurry by, and head to the next main avenue, Tran Nhan Tong, about eight lanes wide of whizzing traffic. On the other side is Lenin Park and Bay Mau Lake.

This street is a little more of a challenge to cross, and I almost chicken out and offer a nearby cyclo some *dong* just to ferry me over. I finally manage to cross, however, and at the entry gate pay 2,500 *dong* to get in. It is a peaceful old park with a high tree canopy overhead and a carefully laid-out grid of pavement in the entrance area. Serpentine swirls of paths snake through the grass leading out to the more remote parts. There are older folks strolling, younger ones playing games of badminton, and, in the secluded spots, teen-agers making out on benches.

The path that leads around this larger lake is more removed from the traffic, and although it is still present, the noise is much fainter. There are tropical gardens, statues, picnic areas and a bright red wooden bridge leading to a little island with a pagoda on it. Large sweeping Banyan trees rim the lake, leaning over the water at precarious angles, and are distinguishable by the unusual roots that dangle down from the higher branches into the water. I stop in a sunny spot and sit on a bench just at the edge of the lake near one of those immense trees. The roots from the branches sweep down, like a girl with long hair gazing at her reflection in the surface of the water, the strands of her hair draping around her face to touch the shimmering surface.

I pull my portable watercolor kit out of my backpack. It was a gift a few years ago, and I have been using it during my travels ever since. Strictly amateur stuff, but I find that by the time I get done painting a scene, the place is so solidly imprinted upon my memory that I hardly need a photograph. There's a little brush, blocks of paint, each about the size of a pencil sharpener, and a water flask, all in a compact little box. I hope that I can get off a handful or so small, postcard-sized paintings on this trip, something to show Lily when she gets older.

I get my supplies set up and am pondering how I'm going to manage painting those unusual roots, when I begin attracting a crowd. I have the lake, some pillars and some of the tree filled in when three young girls come up behind me to observe. They giggle, and one of them can speak a little English. "Where are you from?" she asks.

"I'm American," I reply. On the walk over here, when people asked where I am from and I answered United States, I got a few uncomprehending looks, maybe because I said it too fast. But when I said "American," I got very enthusiastic responses, smiles, and occasionally the comment, "America? I have a cousin in California!"

I have been wondering what response I would receive, what kind of reception I would get as an American in this country, especially up north. At home, when you mention 'Vietnam' to people, more often than not you receive a guarded, even volatile reaction. There is still a lingering feeling of 'we were the good guys, they were the bad guys.' This afternoon in Hanoi, I have only been greeted with positive remarks.

"Oh, *American*! That is very good!" she replies, her eyes widening.

I have brought my Vietnamese phrasebook with me. I first opened it on the plane, and quickly realized what a difficult language it is. Unlike other Asian countries, thanks to the Jesuits, over a hundred years ago the written language was converted to the Roman alphabet instead of the typical character symbols that they used to share with the Chinese, so at least it's familiar in that way to our eyes. But the unusual pronunciations require a vast array of accent marks, dashes, dots and squiggles to indicate how particular letters sound as well as certain combinations of letters, and whether the letters strung together have a pitch that stays the same, goes up, down, dips or breaks. Depending on these marks, for instance, the word '*ba*' could mean three, grandmother, poisoned food, waste, aunt or any. I have no delusions of being able to pick up more than a few handy phrases like hello, thank you and maybe a few food items. Forget grammar and sentence structure. If I get in a jam, at least I will have the phrasebook with me to look something up and to point.

The girl goes through the litany of classroom questions: "What is your name? How old are you? How do you like Vietnam?" I tell her that everywhere I have walked people have been staring.

"Because you are very beautiful," was her reply. "You are lucky, because you are whit...whit...you are white..." she finished. I am embarrassed, and don't know how to reply. The enormous footprint of western culture has left its arrogant mark. Here is an absolutely lovely Asian girl, and she's buying into the commercial ideal of western beauty that none of us, western women included, can live up to. She asks if I have children.

"No, I don't," and I leaf through my Vietnamese phrasebook/dictionary, and can't find the terms for adoption, or orphanage, either.

"Do you have a husband?"

"No, no husband."

Now I have her really stymied. Someone my age just has a husband, that's all there is to it. "You are here with a friend?"

"No, by myself." She looks stunned.

I'm still flipping pages to try to find something that will be able to describe why I am in Vietnam. I find the word for daughter, and point to it in the book. It's pointless for me to try to pronounce the difficult Vietnamese accent marks. "I come to Vietnam to adopt a daughter, a Vietnamese baby."

I'm not sure if she understands the word 'adopt,' but after thinking a moment, she figures it out. "And you will take her back to America?"

"Yes."

Her eyes widen. "She is a very lucky baby!"

By now a crowd of about ten people has formed around us, all of them teenagers. I'm on my bench, the girls are to my right, and the rest are behind us, trying to understand our conversation. We pass the book back and forth to each other, pointing out words and phrases, and laughing until my paints have dried out. I decide to pack up and head back towards my hotel, as it's a bit of a walk. We say goodbye, and she says maybe we'll see each other here at the park again. "Maybe we will," I reply. "It's very pretty here. I'll be coming back."

The crowd disperses and we head off in separate directions. I take a zig-zag route back to the Army Guesthouse, picking some smaller streets that aren't so noisy or hard to cross. I pass children still carrying their backpacks from school, and mothers and grand-mothers greeting them on the street. Women squat curbside with baskets of vegetables, or bunches of tiny red and yellow bananas for sale. I dodge motorbikes being rolled back from the sidewalk, and others that bump quickly over the curb from the street into the newly vacated spaces.

Older men sit on their tiny plastic stools or on crates, engaged in passionate conversation, drinking tea or café. I get the feeling that I could really be walking down the street of any big city, any-where on the planet. Apart from the exotic trappings, like the om-nipresent *non la*, the conical hat made out of rice straw that keeps away the blazing sun, people go about their business pretty much the way they do everywhere. We all hope for the same things. We all laugh. We all revel in companionship. And we all love our children.

Back at the hotel, Rough Guide tells me there is a restaurant nearby that specializes in Hue cuisine. Since I'll be heading down that way in a couple of weeks, I decide to try it out. I'm barely through the hotel gates when one of the cyclo drivers calls out "You go cyclo?" No, I shake my head. And I move my fingers to demonstrate walking.

The cyclo driver maneuvers his vehicle off the curb and wheels it towards me. "You go cyclo! It too late to walk."

"I don't go very far. Cafe Hue. It's very close." I smile, but keep walking.

"Cafe Hue! I know! I know Cafe Hue! I take you there!"

Cafe Hue is only about five blocks away. I am suspicious about how much he would like to charge for such a short trip. Besides, it's still light, and I *like* to walk. "No, no...I go there myself."

A block and a half away, he is still following me. "Missy, missy, I take you Cafe Hue. You no pay for now. I come back for you and show you the city. *Then* you pay."

Hanoi at night by cyclo. It might just give me a chance to see more of the places that I've highlighted in Rough Guide instead of being stuck in my room.

"OK, OK...you can take me to Cafe Hue!"

He comes closer and is beaming. I can now see that he has extensive scars on his face and neck...old healed burns that keep his mouth from closing properly. He has almost no lips. As he rolls the cyclo up to me, he tilts the front forward to bring the foot platform of the cab to the ground. This pops the back wheel of the bicycle off the ground.

"OK! Yes, Cafe Hue! I take you there!" he repeats, as I climb into the cab. He tilts the bicycle back and climbs on to pedal us away.

"What your name?" he asks me, and I reply Ellen. "Ellen," he repeats back to me "Missy Ellen!"

"What's your name?" I ask.

"Phuc" he replies.

"Phuc?" I ask, trying to shape my mouth and lips just the right way.

"Yes, my name is Phuc." It sounds like halfway between 'fook' and, well, you know. How on earth am I going to manage calling him by name for the rest of the night?

As I try to look back at him over my shoulder, I can't see much, as the cyclo has a plasticized fabric cover that drapes down the back and sides, then up over the top like an awning. There is a little fringe sewn along the front edge that dangles down. Through one of the openings between the side and back, I can see the right bicycle handle bar. His hand resting on it is burned as well, and his pinkie and half of his ring finger are missing. I try to picture his face again, and wonder how old he might be. It is hard to tell with the scars. An uninvited thought enters my mind. Perhaps there was some horrible accident during the war. It's hard to keep the 30-year-ago war from coming to mind from time to time, wandering around this city. Perhaps he was a northern soldier...or a child...

and survived the bombings. And now here he is, cheerfully pedaling an American woman around Hanoi in 2001. Let's see…how old would he have to be? I'm not sure that I'll get up the nerve to ask how those scars came to be. Would it be rude? Would the Vietnamese consider it rude? For now, I leave the question alone.

At our first intersection, one without a traffic light, he barely slows. We make a left turn, a wide, curving arc onto a main street, with motorbikes and cars, bicycles and other cyclos swerving around us. I fight the urge to close my eyes, but my legs instinctively contract and I push both feet into the floorboard. Breathe, I tell myself.

We pass a construction site that has a few workers winding up for the day. They don't have a wheelbarrow or forklift to move a pile of leftover bricks. Instead, I see the men carrying the bricks in baskets on their heads. One fellow, who is thin and wiry and looks about fifty, balances his full basket and holds the rim with one hand, while he squats down, lifts the single wayward brick above his head, places it in the basket, straightens up, and continues on through to the back of the work site.

Two more right turns and we are in front of Cafe Hue. Phuc eases the cyclo up to the curb and tilts it forward so I can climb out. I look at my watch. It is 5:45.

"I be here until 6:30, then we go see city." I tell him. I notice that I have started dropping some of the words from my sentences.

"6:30! OK! OK! I be here at 6:30!"

At the open-air restaurant, I order spring rolls, banana flower salad and asparagus-crab soup. The menu is printed in Vietnamese with English and French translations, and a scan of the rest of it doesn't reveal anything terribly scary (Rough Guide talks about dog meat being a Northern delicacy!), although I'm not sure if I would ever give the snake-head fish a try.

At 6:30, Phuc is nowhere to be seen. Ten minutes later I start back for the hotel. When I round the final corner, I see him kicked back in the cab of his cyclo, chatting with the other drivers. When he sees me, he jumps up, hops on his bike seat, and pedals down to meet me.

"We go cyclo now! Where you want to go?"

Nothing about standing me up at the restaurant. I pull out my Rough Guide map, and look at the places that I have highlighted. Kimbo Cafe for dessert, and then Hang Gai, the silk district.

"You know Kimbo Cafe?" I ask.

"Yes! Yes! I know Kimbo Cafe! Very popular...many tourist go there. Very famous!"

Off we go to Kimbo Cafe. Rough Guide says that you can get fresh French parties there, as well as home-made yogurt with fruit. Its claim to fame is that actress Catherine Deneuve once complimented the owner on the quality of his yogurt. It has been a landmark ever since.

It starts to get dark, and the city is becoming illuminated with streetlights, neon signs and bright shop lights. After a few more seemingly close calls in the traffic, I finally relax and trust Phuc to do the driving.

Kimbo Cafe is at a major intersection of five large streets. With a little maneuvering, Phuc has me at the curb again. Everywhere there are people, motorbikes, and vendors with baskets of fruit displayed on the sidewalk. Women, their heads covered by their *non la*, carry their *giong ganh* (pronounced 'yung gen') over their shoulders, the long pole with a shallow basket hanging off of each end that is familiar to me from Asian artwork. Out of these baskets, they have for sale bananas, oranges, or maybe even a little lit stove on one side, with bowls, spoons, veggies and chopped greens on the other, ready to serve up a bowl of hot noodle soup.

There is a grace to the way they carry this *giong ganh*, with their body turned so the pole rests on the forward shoulder, the pole sticking out to the front and behind them, one hand grasping the pole in front of them, the other in back. Otherwise they wouldn't be able to maneuver on the sidewalk. Their step is a glide-and-bounce that makes the two ends bob up and down, and I imagine the spring created makes it a little easier to carry. When she is ready to switch sides, the woman pauses and drops her front shoulder while rolling the pole to the opposite side around behind her neck, assuming the same position only with the other shoulder forward now. This apparently is a major form of transport in Vietnam…I have seen it everywhere since I have arrived.

The open storefront of Kimbo Café is half-way covered by a glass case. Lined up neatly inside are rows of baguettes, croissants, hot savory pies and glazed fruit pastries of the sort that you would see along the *Boulvard St. Michel* in Paris. Inside, I take a seat and order yogurt with fresh fruit. While I am waiting, I go back up to the cases to pick out a few things to bring back to the hotel room. Chocolate croissants, a glazed apple tart, and a few cookies. My yogurt comes in a tall, slender glass, with sliced fresh strawberries, mangoes and papaya, a long spoon and a bowl of sugar. Madam Catherine was right.

Phuc has waited at the corner this time. Carrying my bag of goodies, I climb in and say "Next, Hang Gai!"

The Old Town part of Hanoi is a zigzag of streets, and the shops also are arranged by the wares they sell. Hang Gai is the silk street. There is also Hang Bac, Hang Quat, and Hang Da, where you can find lacquer-ware, brass, religious items, shoes and embroidered items such as tablecloths and napkins.

Phuc leaves me off at the corner, and I start out by window-shopping. Halfway down the first block, there is a break in the shops, and in the space is an enormous ancient tree with deeply patterned bark. It is hard to say whether the shops are built into the tree's convoluted trunk or if the tree has grown into the walls of the shops. I imagine that a little of both happened over the period of many years, many decades probably. It is obviously a place of ritual: inserted in the cracks and crevices of the trunk from the base in the sidewalk to up over my head are hundreds and hundreds of stubs from incense sticks. A few fresh sticks burn as well, and they send their wispy perfume out to be carried away by the breeze caused by the passing motorbikes.

Shop workers stand in front of their establishments trying to usher people in the door. "Very good prices!" they say, "Very beautiful!" pointing to the goods in their window. The larger shops have racks of clothes that you can try on. But there are small shops that have only a few sample items hanging on their walls, and bolts and bolts of cloth, brightly colored and patterned silk, stacked on shelves from floor to ceiling. They tailor-make everything they sell. I choose one such shop to stop at, and its young proprietress is quick to pull down a few *ao dais* from their hooks on the wall.

"My clothes much cheaper, because my shop is small," she says. Her shop consists of one wall hung with samples, an aisle less than three feet wide that goes back about thirty feet, and the left wall that is nothing but neatly folded and stacked silk all the way up to the ceiling tiles.

"I use the same tailors as the big shops, but my prices are better. I give you good price!" Her English is better than Phuc's, and she doesn't have the habit that he does of repeating things multiple times back to you. Her name is Thuy, pronounced 'twee.' She is very pretty, with an animated smiling face. Her long black hair is pulled back into a pony-tail.

"I will be here for two months...I don't want to buy anything yet...I'll have to carry it around."

"That's OK! I keep for you here at the shop until you want to pick it up! What are you in Vietnam that much time for?"

I tell her about adopting Lily. She understands the concepts of 'adopt' and 'orphan,' so I don't have to struggle trying to communicate that. She too is very surprised that I'm here all alone, *and* that I am doing such a thing without a husband. Then she pauses.

"Maybe it's better that way! You do not have to take care of a husband too!" She cocks her head to one side and gives me a knowing smile, her dark eyes sparkling and laughing. It's a girl moment...some things are universal, regardless of the culture.

I smile back and turn to look at her samples, running my fingers over the smooth shiny surfaces. "How much for the *ao dai*?" I ask.

"*Ao dai*?" Thuy pronounces it 'Ow Zye' "Twenty-four dollars, both for top and pants. Very good quality!" and she displays for me the work on the seams of the samples.

"And if I buy several *ao dai*?" I say, copying her 'ow zye.'

"If you buy more than three, twenty dollars each."

Swiftly she pulls some bolts part-way out of the stacks, and drapes the fabric over her arm to show me the sheen. I finger some of the fabric, gravitating towards the greens and coppers.

"We can do zipper in front or side, or elastic waist. High collar and closing down front or diagonally across shoulder. Your choice of fabric buttons. Whatever you want!" Like Phuc, most of her statements sound like they end with exclamation points.

In spite of the fact that I know I should look around more, and bargain a little more ruthlessly, I can't resist and order two *ao dais* and two extra pairs of pants. I tell her I want to order some for friends back home, but need to e-mail for measurements.

"Yes! OK!" she says as she pulls out her tape and stretches it between my neck and shoulder, from shoulder to wrist, neck to waist, waist to calf, calling the numbers out to her assistant, who looks like her younger sister. While she is doing that, we talk about me traveling to Vietnam and my adopting Lily.

"Lucky baby," she says. "Where is the baby now?"

I tell her Lang Son, trying several ways to pronounce it before she understands where I'm talking about.

"Lang Son! Oh, it is very poor in Lang Son. People very poor there..."

'Lank Sun' it sounds like when she says it. Both words are very clipped and even-toned. I practice a few times.

Here I am in Vietnam, a relatively poor country, and the people in this city, Hanoi, are by Western standards, pretty poor, and *they* consider the people who live in Lang Son province very poor. I'm wondering what I will see when I head up north in a few days.

I give Thuy $40 US as a deposit and pause at the doorway and pick out about a dozen silk scarves and shawls to bring home for gifts. Four dollars each! These she bundles up for me, then climbs up a ladder at the back of the shop, moves a ceiling tile, and stashes them above. When she climbs back down we say goodbye, and she tells me to come back in two days to try on my outfits.

ONCE I AM BACK OUT on the street, I turn to find Phuc. It's about eight-thirty, and I can't wait to settle into the cyclo seat. I spot him parked with some other cyclo drivers again, shooting the breeze, but he hops up quickly once he sees me at the corner. He has been safeguarding my pastries as well.

"Can you drive around now and show me a little of the city? That's enough walking for me," I tell him as he rolls the cyclo up.

"You see city! OK! OK!"

He pedals me around, not past any monuments or statues or famous places from what I can tell. Instead I see people coming home at the end of the day carrying their groceries, children playing and stores closing up. A light mist is falling. The blackness of the pavement glistens and reflects the streetlights, the shop lights and the headlights of the motorbikes like shimmering stars. The women carrying their *giong ganh* walk a little lighter, their baskets now empty. The smell of wet pavement mingles with the aroma of cooking vegetables, noodles and fish sauce. Motorbike horns beep, the rubber tires of Phuc's cyclo splash through tiny puddles, and the rhythm of his feet pedaling me forward causes the cyclo canopy to shake and sway gently. The chopped musical sound of the Vietnamese language from people that we pass blends with it all into a city medley.

Phuc carries on a conversation of his own, not waiting for any response from me. He repeats himself over and over, mostly telling me that it is very good that I am American, it is very good that I visit, that he has met many very nice Americans, and that this little girl is a very lucky baby.

BACK AT THE HOTEL, I'm ready for bed and am reading through Rough Guide again. Lang Son, it tells me, has a couple of serviceable hotels, and is mostly used as a stopping over point for travelers going on to China. The area around the border has changed hands between Vietnam and China many times over the centuries, and many of the people are ethnically Chinese. Forget about quaint villages and monuments and temples to visit, it tells me. Lang Son is a practical, industrial, commercial city. But it doesn't matter. Lily is there.

What is her story? What is her mother's story? I cannot think about one without the other. For Lily to be my daughter, there must be a tragic other story that brings her to me. Perhaps an unwed mother in a country that does not accept such things? Vietnam is not like China with a one child only rule, so parents don't abandon girls in favor of boys due to a restriction from the government. What brought her mother, her birth mother, to the decision to give her up, to decide that she could not care for this little girl?

Chapter opening photograph: Bay Mau Lake, Hanoi, Vietnam

Chapter 2

AT JUST BEFORE FIVE A.M., it is still dark. Stepping out onto the patio of my hotel room, my face is splashed with a cool moisture-laden breeze. The droplets of water are large and suspended in the air, exploding on my skin when they make contact. Above my head, there is a bird flying. I don't see him, I hear him. He is large and circles heavily, calling out an incessant *"zhree! zhree!"* The bird and I are the only ones awake.

I am bothered by the dream that I have awakened from. In the dream I have Lily with me, but I keep forgetting her everywhere, at shopping malls, in cars... At the beginning of the dream, Lily is placed in my arms. She has that same solemn-looking face that I know so well from the photograph. She calls for her me-ma, who I understood to be her grandmother. I put her down to go get something from another room, and when she is out of my sight, I very distinctly hear a voice call: "you are *not* my mother."

I go back inside and sit on the bed, nibbling my croissants and drinking tea that I have brewed using water from the hotpot that the hotel has placed in the room. I wonder what will happen when she first sees me. At home, I have been a member of an Internet newsgroup called APV, Adoptive Parents of Vietnam, since July. The members have been an invaluable resource in this process, providing information from travel tips to issues that can arise in multi-cultural families, to help in completing paperwork. I even found out about Binh through the list, from someone who had used him to adopt her own two little daughters. I have read on the list that often with Asian adoptions, you are probably the first Caucasian person that the child has ever seen, and that it might take a few days for them to not be afraid of you. Expect them to cry, to want to go back to the person, the *Asian* person, who had been holding them.

I *will* be your mother, little girl. I will earn that title by bringing you into my life and sharing it with you, by teaching you about the world and the beautiful things in it, and by hopefully bringing you happiness and joy and lots of smiles.

It is still a surreal feeling, this idea that in a matter of days I will meet my daughter. All the paperwork and preparation up until now has been like a dream that I will wake up from. It seems that one morning I will find that all this isn't really happening and I will go on with the life that I have always known. But it's not a dream. I am awake, and *this* is reality, this room on the other side of the world, these breaths that I am breathing. The preparation and waiting is all finished and there's nothing else for me to do other than to meet Lily and begin a new, totally changed life...together. Have I made the right choice? Will I be able to do this on my own? What will I lose from my old life? Will I regret this? Have I put too much ex-pectation on her? What *are* my expectations? Will I be a good mother? How can I be sure that I will fall in love with her? Or that she will fall in love with me? How hard will this be? I close my eyes, trying to quiet the questions ricocheting around in my head and do my breathing. I concentrate on the thought, on the feeling that this is just a part of the path that I am on. Do we choose our lives or do our lives choose us? This choice, this path, will open up an entire-ly different world for me, and I have no idea what to expect, no idea what that world looks like...I've never seen it before.

At six a.m. I hear a recording of a trumpet playing a Vietnamese form of reveille. It seems the Army Guest House gets its name by its proximity to barracks of some sort. By six-fifteen I am on my way out the door, and it is just getting light enough for an early morning walk. The rain has continued during the night and the road glistens. The cyclo drivers are not yet at their usual post across from the gate, and I head out in a totally new direction, towards Hoan Kiem Lake, which serves as the center of the Old Town.

The streets are just starting to get busy with the early morning crowd. On one of the narrow streets, an older woman is coming towards me, carrying her *giong ganh* laden with vegetables. Her back is curved forward like a question mark from the weight of carrying this load for years of days. She wears her *non la*, secured under her chin by a strip of fabric, has on a dark plain tunic and pants, and is shoeless. As she nears me, I hear her feet make a slapping noise against the damp pavement. Her feet are splayed wide and flat, the toes separated. I imagine that's what feet look like if you don't wear shoes...ever. Slap, slap, slap against the tiny puddles that linger in the road.

A little further on, I come upon two women selling bananas out of their baskets. They point to them, silently asking me if I want to buy any. I shake my head no, then a few steps later decide I would enjoy eating a few in my hotel room later, so I turn back. I point to the bananas, ask them "how much?" in English for the small bunch that I have picked out, and hold out a pen and my journal for her to write down the numbers in *dong*. She writes 50,000. "*Dong*!?" I ask, and she nods yes.

She's asking over three dollars for six bananas, when that would probably buy her whole load for the day! I'm still trying to get used to doing monetary conversions in my head. There's probably a little over a kilo of bananas there — I'm trying to get used to thinking in kilos, too. I draw a line through her 50,000 and write below it 15,000, which she counters by crossing it out and writing 20,000.

Still probably too much, but the difference is only about thirty cents to me. That same thirty cents makes so much more of a difference in her life. I nod OK, and hand over two 10,000 *dong* notes, Ho Chi Minh's face staring out at us from the front of the bills.

Before I leave, I take out my digital camcorder and point to it and then to them. They seem OK with the idea, and I shoot about thirty seconds of video of the ladies and their baskets. Then I play it back on the small screen for them to see. When they see their faces, they point back and forth to each other and laugh. They are entertained, and when it's done I pack the camera away. One of them holds out her hand, palm up. She wants to be paid, it seems, for starring briefly in my movie, and the other one follows suit. I should have seen that one coming. I pull out a couple of 2,000 *dong* notes and give one to each, shaking my head when they reach out for more. I had planned on trying to get lots of live-action shots at markets and on the streets, but it looks like that might be too expensive a proposition. Perhaps my camera will remain packed away except when I'm taking footage of Lily and the adoption ceremony, which are the main reasons I bought it anyway.

I FIND THE DONG XUAN MARKET by chance, having gotten lost down a few narrow, crooked streets when I couldn't find any street signs. It is said to be the largest covered market in this part of Hanoi. It is now past six-thirty, and I am perusing the outdoor market that is behind Dong Xuan. It is crammed full of people. There are awnings draped over the street, strung between buildings on either side, with stalls and tables underneath.

It starts simply enough, stalls heaped with fruits and veggies. As I wade deeper into the rows of tables, the contents progress to seafood, dried fish and fresh ones that are flapping out onto the street from shallow metal pans, only to be lifted back onto the pans again. Then comes the poultry, live chickens and ducks scrunched tightly into bamboo and wire cages, others in the process of being plucked, disemboweled, de-headed and de-footed, even bled, with their wings still flapping, into bowls. Congealed duck blood is a local delicacy.

Beef and pork is being cut from large slabs into smaller pieces, while various innards, brains and intestines are being carried, sliding around on plastic trays. I try to take tiny, shallow breaths, not wanting to take the smell and molecules of offal, dried fish and sewage too deeply into my lungs. Thank God it's drizzling so my shoes will, somewhat, wash off. Now I understand why Asians have the custom of taking their shoes off at the door!

After a cozy squeeze between the clothing vendors, padded bras, pantyhose, and winter gear (at sixty-five degrees, this is winter in Hanoi!), I pop out on the far side of the market, and a little breeze pushes away the market smell behind me.

In a few more blocks, I come upon Hoan Kiem Lake, which at this hour is shrouded in drifting veils of mist. The pagoda and bridge nearby seem to hover on a cloud, and the Banyan trees drape their roots like fingers trailing in the water. There are paths and grassy areas that ring the lake, and many of the older inhabitants of Hanoi are there doing calisthenics and some form of Tai Chi exercise. A blond-haired, blue-eyed, European-looking couple jog by wearing shorts and tank tops. Otherwise, the lake at this early hour belongs to the older generation, and they pay very little attention to me. I find a secluded bench to sit on and watch the city wake up and stretch.

BEFORE I MAKE IT all the way back to the hotel, the rising sun has burned off any mist or drizzle that still hung in the air. I stop at a cafe with sidewalk tables and order cafe *sua* ('soo-AH'), the ubiquitous morning drink of Vietnam. It is made of strong, French-style coffee served in a demitasse cup with a half-inch layer of sweetened condensed milk sunk on the bottom. Rough Guide says that this tradition started decades ago when there was no refrigeration available, yet the French colonials still wanted milk in their coffee. The canned milk would keep in the Vietnamese climate.

I dip the slender spoon in to stir it up, the ribbon of milk drizzling down from the end as I lift it out of the coffee, drawing swirling, sinking circles on the surface, light on dark. It tastes strong and sweet, and the tiny cup empties quickly. I order one more.

This is a place that I spotted last night while I was eating dinner. Right across the street, this Café Pho is a hip and trendy joint. It is now eight-thirty, and young, well-dressed professionals are coming and going. They are too hip to be caught giving me curious glances. Some of the men are in suits with shirts but no ties. Women, I notice, don't wear skirts or dresses in Vietnam. Never. At this place, they wear nice pantsuits. And there are leather shoes. The teens hanging out nearby wear brand-name sneakers — well, probably knock-off brand name. In shop windows I have seen Nike and Adidas, Reebok and Asics, with price tags the equivalent of around six dollars U.S. But this nice footwear is limited to a small portion of the population. Almost everyone else I have seen wears plastic sandals, children and grownups alike. It is the footwear of the people squatting along the sidewalks, sitting on plastic stools, eating soup and drinking cafe *sua*. On the people who whiz by on their scooters. On the children as they go to school. Except for the few, like the woman this morning, who wore none. Very practical, I guess, as it rains so much here, and you never have to worry about your feet, never have to worry about getting your shoes wet. They're just *feet*.

JUST BEFORE TEN-THIRTY, I walk into the hotel lobby with my packet of documents and see that Binh is already there. There are six families on the far side of the lobby near the Christmas tree. Caucasian couples, with carriages and strollers, holding infants. I don't have time for a closer look right now, but I'm sure that I'll get a chance later. Binh motions me out to the SUV while he finishes a call on the hotel phone. I join a dark-haired, dark-eyed man about ten years older than myself in the back seat, and as I climb in I say hello.

"Hello," he replies hesitantly and with an accent. European, but I'm not sure from where.

"Do you speak English?" I ask, and he shakes his head. "Parlez Francaise?" I try again. Perhaps he's French, or at least can speak a little French.

It turns out that his name is Mario, and he is Italian. Between some French, English and a little pantomime, he tells me that he's here with his wife to adopt a little girl, three months old. They will be keeping her Vietnamese name, Lien, and he is going with us today to turn in the paperwork for her Vietnamese passport. They have already had their adoption ceremony, so they should be going home in a few days.

Our first stop is for Mario, and I wait in the car with the driver while Binh and Mario go inside. About twenty minutes later, they come out. Mario tells me that the papers will be ready in two days, and then—he shoots his hand out and up, like an airplane taking off. They are lucky! They'll be home for Christmas.

The next stop is for me. We pull up to the local government office that certifies paperwork, and Binh and I get out. Mario decides that he doesn't want to wait in the car, so he joins us as well. We enter a room that is crowded with Vietnamese men and women. Some are sitting in seats, some are filling out paperwork at tables. Most are pushing and shoving their way up to a counter, reaching over each other and trying to slide fistfuls of documents to the workers on the other side of the glass. Waiting in line, Vietnam-style. Binh asks me for my paperwork and enters the fray. Within moments he has passed my papers to the other side of the glass. He rejoins me and says for me to take a seat until my name is called. This takes about twenty minutes, and Mario and I watch as the confusion continues, with no effort on anyone's part to bring a little order to the scene. Behind the glass, the workers stoically receive, examine and pass on to other workers circulating behind them the stacks and stacks of documents.

The paperwork that Binh has passed through the window, my sixty-page *dossier*, is all of my required documents, in English with Vietnamese translations. There are forms from the U.S. INS (Immigration and Naturalization Service). Forms from the State of Virginia for the government of Vietnam. Recently certified copies of my birth certificate from New York City, divorce decree from South Carolina, my application for international adoption of an orphan, a current medical exam, my police criminal history record (or, rather, the statement that I have no criminal record), a child protective services clearance, a commitment letter stating that I agree to send annual updates on the child until she reaches 18 to the involved province, a financial statement from my accountant...

For months I have compiled documents and organized them in an accordion file. Almost every day something was either coming in or going out in the mail. I had to be especially attentive since I am doing an independent adoption, which means that I am doing it without going through an adoption agency. No one was checking up on me on my end to make sure that I was gathering the proper paperwork. The extra effort on my part paid off in the bottom line: agency adoption estimates for international adoptions start at around $20,000 and go up from there. Without paying agency fees, my costs should end up being half that.

Call it fate or serendipity or just plain luck, but my documents all came and went and were returned again in record time. I started the paperwork path in August, and just two weeks ago was Fed Ex-ing copies of the whole thing to Binh in Hanoi to have it all translated into Vietnamese. Under four months. There are people who wait a year, two or even more for their dream to come true. I am quietly thankful. This must be, *must* be meant to be.

I don't hear my name called, but Binh jumps up and motions me to the counter, pushing people aside for me until I reach the window. A woman has my dossier, and she is carefully examining each and every page, every certified copy. Where there are notary stamps with a raised seal, she is careful to run her fingertips lightly over it, as if she were reading Braille, making sure that it is authentic. She flips back and forth between a few pages, checking I don't know what against each other. A time or two, she pauses to look up at me, then glances back down to the pages without saying a word. She finally looks up to Binh, and says something to him in Vietnamese.

"You need to give her two million four hundred thousand *dong* for the certifications." He tells me.

This is about $160 U.S., and I'm glad that I stopped by the ATM and got *dong* out this morning at a bank by Hoan Kiem Lake. Apparently, for each certified document that I have from the U.S., this office needs to certify that each piece of paper has been certified *properly*. I count out twenty-four faces of Uncle Ho, receive a receipt, and we head out the door. Binh says the papers will be ready tomorrow.

Dropping me off in front of the Army Guesthouse, Binh tells me to be in the lobby at eight-thirty tomorrow morning so we can go pick up the papers.

I ask him if all is still on for us to go to Lang Son on Wednesday. "Yes," he says. "We will go to Lang Son on Wednesday." Across the street, Phuc sees me, and waves, making sure that I know that he is there waiting for our next excursion. A *nap*, however, is what is waiting for me, in my hotel room.

WITH SOME REST and a bit of fruit under my belt, I head out into the afternoon for some more sightseeing. By the time I reach the gate, Phuc is half-way across the street with his cyclo. None of the other drivers have budged, or try to signal me their way. Apparently there is some 'cyclo driver code,' an understanding that once someone is your customer, you have continuing dibs on them.

"I want to go sightseeing," I tell Phuc. "Same price? Fifteen thousand *dong* per hour?" This is the price that we settled on the other night. It seems easier than doing things trip by trip.

"OK, OK! I take you, Missy Ellen! What you want to go see?"

"I want to see all the things that the tourists come to see. All the famous stuff."

As we take off down the street, Phuc starts up his ongoing, repetitive form of conversation. "You go cyclo with Phuc...I take you! When you go to Lang Son for your daughter, you will be happy! I know! I know! I have two children! Children make you very happy! She is very lucky baby! It is very good that she will be in America! I have met very nice Americans!" It is hard to answer him even if I could get a word in, as he really doesn't ask any questions, so finally I stop trying and let him chatter away.

Phuc takes me to see the Temple of Literature, where hundreds of years ago Confucian scholars studied. It is a walled sanctuary within Hanoi, and encompasses several city blocks. Inside the entrance is a methodical grid of paved pathways set around even rows of raised rectangular ponds. The green full-moons of lily pads sleep lightly on the surface of the water. There are statues and fountains of fish and turtles. The trees around the perimeter reach and stretch their branches overhead, as if trying to hold the city back and cradle this oasis under their protective fingers.

Next, Phuc takes me to Ho Chi Minh's mausoleum. I have to walk a short distance, as cyclos aren't allowed on the wide avenue that circles the complex. In front there is yet another evenly laid out weave of pavement. White cement walkways reflect the sunlight, and horizontally and vertically divide perfectly manicured squares of grass, each about three paces long. There are no trees to hold back the city here, and the whole expanse is wide and open and flows several hundred yards in each direction. Behind this mandala rise several dozen steps that lead up to a gray columned building that houses Ho Chi Minh's embalmed body sequestered in a glass display case. Today I decide to pass on a viewing as the weather is so lovely; I'd rather be outside. I'll have a chance to return some other day.

Our last stop is a divided road that follows the shore of West Lake. Large ancient trees march down the grassy median, and on the east side of the road shimmers West Lake. To the west is Truc Bach Lake, where there is a sign telling me that during the war, American aggressors were shot down over these waters. There are also several pagodas along the shore, and I visit Tran Quoc, whose towering levels resemble a wedding cake, and which dates back to the sixth century.

At each stop, there are children, teenagers and women selling t-shirts, postcards, wooden frog percussion instruments, and miniature *non la*. "Missy! Missy! You buy (fill-in-the-blank)??" No, I would *not* like a t-shirt with 'Uncle Ho' on the front, or the bright red t-shirt with the gold star on it signifying the Vietnamese flag. It reminds me of the Hardees logo back home. They are persistent, they follow you, and they don't take no for an answer. You can't look at them, smile at them, show weakness or indecision, or slow your steps, otherwise your way will be blocked—you will be engulfed.

It's been over three hours, and I finally tell Phuc to take us back to the hotel. When we get there, I find a gathering of families in the lobby. Several couples are there: the Italians, including Mario and his wife, and a new couple I haven't met before from Ireland. John and Deirdra have a little girl, and are also waiting on her passport. They'll be home for Christmas, too. There is one little boy, and all the rest are girls. Other than John and Deirdre's Aoefe ('ee-fah'), who is one year old, all of the other babies are quite young, around three to four months of age. A few tiny heads are bare, exposing very short, black, prickly hair. Other heads are capped with perfect, clean little hats to match perfect, clean little outfits. There are binkies, blankets, strollers, rattles, bottles, cameras and diaper bags. Lien happily sucks on Mario's fat thumb. The other parents hover and circle, trying to anticipate the next desire or need, trying to comfort at first cry, clumsy and delirious in the newness of parenthood. My time is coming. Only two more days. Actually, one more day and two nights, but who's counting?

I exit to "goodbyes" and "*Ciaos*" and on the way to my room I stop to sift through a stack of menus at the front desk. It seems that all of the restaurants deliver, not just pizza places. I abscond to my room with a menu for Moca Cafe, a bistro-like place that Phuc passed near Notre Dame cathedral. I place an order for vegetarian Indian food and for about five bucks I get *samosas*, *naan*, rice, veggie curry and sliced fresh mango and papaya brought straight to room 102. At least with this meal, I don't have to worry about bumping into the dreaded *nuoc mam*, fish sauce.

Fish sauce is sort of the national condiment of Vietnam, like ketchup is for America. Unfortunately, just the smell of it makes me want to retch. I found this out back home several months ago when I ate at a Thai restaurant. They had to remove a dish of green papaya salad from the table after I almost heaved across it after putting a big gob of it in my mouth. I managed to make it to the bathroom to spit it down the toilet before that happened. Rough Guide has since told me what fish sauce was made of. Basically, you throw a bunch of fish—head, guts and all — into a barrel of brine, and let it rot in the sun for a month or two. Then you siphon off the goo that results and bottle it. There are companies that vie for the honor of having the best fish sauce, and Phu Quoc Island, an island south of the mainland, produces copious amount of it, grading it like olive oil. After that first dramatic experience, I can now determine if even the smallest amount was used in the preparation of a dish, usually in the steam released shortly after it hits the table. One thing that I fear in the coming weeks is that it will be used liberally and overwhelmingly in everything that I am served.

THE NEXT MORNING when Binh comes to pick me up, it is raining. Sometimes a drizzle, but mostly in torrents. On the streets there are just as many motorbikes whizzing by today as on previous dry days, but now their drivers are wearing plastic rain ponchos. If there is a passenger, they are usually stuffed up under the poncho of the driver in front of them. Plastic-sandaled feet are wet, glistening and dirty from road splatter.

The beeping of horns is a soundtrack to the weave and dance through the puddles as I peer through the window of the SUV. I hold my breath as a Toyota and a girl on a bicycle seem to be on a course to occupy the same little bit of street at the same time when they each come to a jarring halt just inches from each other. There is a pause, then both girl and driver break into laughter as other motorists swerve around them. At a stoplight, I glance at a young couple idling next to us on their motorbike. Ponchos cover their heads, shoulders and arms, and flap loosely around their lower bodies. A hand reaches back to caress the place between her blue jean-clad legs, and an instant later they both turn their heads to see me seeing them. Startled and embarrassed, I recoil, hoping the tint of the glass window can camouflage my unintended witness.

I wonder about what I have expected to find in this country and its people. My experience with Vietnam has been limited to two things. Firstly, the War, and the media, images and psychology that revolve, vibrate and swell around it. Although I am too young to remember much of the war as it was actually happening, the ripples created by it for the next decades were inescapable for my generation. And those born just before me lived it…or in some cases didn't.

The other exposure that I have had to Vietnam was when I became interested in the teachings of Vietnamese monk-author-teacher-peace activist Thich Nhat Hanh in the 1990s. Through his books, I learned about rising above the frenzy of our Western life and cultivating the presence of peace in myself. I challenged the goals and desires that I had accepted as crucial to my happiness, and focused my consciousness on what I *really* needed in my life to be happy. I learned about Mindfulness, paying attention to the details of living my life as it unfolds, and how living in the present moment is the only place that you can find happiness. I learned that all of this is not so easy, but that you get better at it with practice.

I attended two summer retreats at Plum Village, Thich Nhat Hanh's home in Southwest France. *Thay's* ('*Thay*,' pronounced 'tie,' means teacher in Vietnamese) profound personal presence and teachings were magnetic and inspiring. I lived for several weeks amidst this community of mostly Vietnamese monks and nuns, with their shaved heads and clad in brown robes, and observed them practicing mindfulness in their walking, eating, working and relationships with others. It opened up to me a whole new way of looking at my life. In Plum Village, whenever a bell chimes or the phone rings or a gong sounds, everything pauses for three breaths. Every person stops what they are doing to take three deep, slow inhalations. This is their opportunity to remember to bring their full awareness to what they are doing at that moment, and to appreciate the subtle joy in it, in their life, in the world around them.

So now I am in Hanoi, the capital of Vietnam for most of the past thousand years, and of the North when our young men were here fighting. Did I expect to see constant physical reminders of what was wrought here thirty years ago? That there would be lingering, thinly-veiled, accusatory glances towards me from those who remember, those who haven't moved on? After all, to them, we were the bad guys. Or did I expect to see throngs of peaceful smiling people going about their day calmly and without hurry, bowing to those they passed, breathing three times while waiting at a stoplight? I tried to avoid placing pre-conceived notions on what I would find, but it is truly difficult not to. At the same time, it is impossible to reconcile these two diverse images in my mind.

The reality is that since I have arrived in Vietnam I have been struck most by the overwhelming busy-ness of everyone. There is frantic rushing to and fro to get to the next stops, to make the next appointment, to arrive at some other destination in their life other than where they are right now. Not so different from what I have left back at home half a world away.

But I have felt nothing but welcome and friendliness from the people that I have met, enthusiasm even. And I have felt completely safe. I am a curiosity and stand out at all times, but, other than the goods-hawkers, who can be tiresome, and the stoic, ultra-professional government clerk, everyone has had a smile for me.

My papers are retrieved from the office in half an hour, and the rain varies between drizzle and driving for the rest of the day. I decide to spend it lingering around the hotel, napping, reading, writing in my journal, visiting when the families come out, and basically having a lazy time of it. That evening I hop on the lobby computer to send my first e-mail home.

Subj: Greetings from Hanoi!
Date:12/11/01 7:43:12 PM
From: Efitz
To: Vietnam Group
Sent from the Internet (Details)

Hello everybody!

I have made it safe and sound to Vietnam, and have spent the past couple of days turning in paperwork, getting it certified by our Embassy and the Vietnam Consulate, and doing a little sightseeing while waiting for them to do their processing. We have Internet access here at the hotel, but tonight's my last night in Hanoi, as I head up to Lang Son tomorrow to meet Lily!

Excited? I'll say! There are six families in this hotel from Italy that all have adopted, and they are wandering around with their babies waiting for their final paperwork processing. Not sure if I'll be able to get in touch while I'm in Lang Son, so I'll fill you all in when I get back. I enjoyed playing peek-a-boo on the long flight to Seoul, Korea with a few little ones...practicing!

The first day, which was nice and sunny, I took a walk and came up with two words to describe Hanoi: Cacophonous Bedlam. And I thought Naples, Italy, was bad! My New York training in crossing streets just touches the tip of the iceberg here, as traffic rules are loose at best. There are countless cars, scooters, buses, trucks and cyclos (rickshaw-like contraptions with a cart with a seat on front, pushed by a bicycle) zipping around at all times. I have taped one cyclo journey on my new camcorder for those interested in the experience when I get back. So far, only one minor collision, after which my driver gave the scooter driver what-for in Vietnamese!

I've been doing some shopping (guess where everyone's next birthday and Christmas presents are coming from??), and have ordered a couple of custom tailored *ao dais* (traditional dress) from a silk shop. "For you missy, good price!"

Beautiful stuff! Want to get a few things for Lily too, and have our first "family photo" taken in Vietnamese garb.

The food is great, as long as I stay away from the fish sauce, and there are little coffee houses everywhere. I had a gruesome experience at an open-air market, where I dodged live and dead animals, various organs sliding across plastic trays, duck blood being gathered to make a special delicacy (congealed duck blood), and all of the accompanying goop on the sidewalks. NOW I know why they take their shoes off at the front door!

Anyway, it is truly a different world. I plan to spend a week in Lang Son, and can visit with Lily every day. After that, while I am waiting for the province to process my paperwork, I might take a couple of short trips, the first to Sa Pa in the mountains, and then to Ha Long Bay on the coast. Those areas are supposed to be very beautiful and will be a great departure from the insanity of the city. Then maybe a pop over to Bangkok, Thailand, or take a tour to Angkor Wat in Cambodia. We'll see how it goes.

Hope everyone is well, and gearing up for the holidays! I'll miss having my own tree set up in the corner of my living room. Lots of Christmas decorations here, by the way!

Love, Ellen

IN MY ROOM, I try to rest. I try to breathe. I try to meditate. I fail miserably at all. Tomorrow. Tomorrow I leave for Lang Son. Tomorrow I meet my daughter. Daughter. What a word. It means more than child, or baby. It implies a *relationship*. "This is my little girl." Sounds very matter-of-fact, and makes her sound like a very separate little being. Try: "This is my *daughter*," however. That somehow makes us a part of each other, and what we will share between us is special and sacred and *big*. I've never had that and I can only imagine what it will be like, and maybe I'm putting too much pressure on this already, and my child, my daughter, will be mentally disturbed because of the unrealistic expectations from her demanding mother and *maybe I'm thinking too damn much*!! Somehow I'll figure out this mommy thing, and she and I will be just fine with neither of us spending a fortune on therapy some years down the road.

An image washes over me and sweeps away any other thought or question. I see two faces next to each other, looking back at me. One is fair with freckles, one is tawny. One has hazel eyes, one dark. Black hair next to auburn. But both faces have smiles on them.

Chapter opening photograph: Buddah, Hue, Vietnam

二

Chapter 3

December 13th

THE LIGHT ON MY INDIGLO wristwatch lights up a fraction of a second before the first beep sounds. I have been lying still in the dark, listening to the silence. It reverberates solidly, palpably between my eardrums and the walls of the room. Beneath me, I feel the pressure of the mattress. On top of me, the motel-room scratchy bedspread that has not quite managed to warm or comfort me. Not *my* bed. Not *my* home. I play a mental game with myself: Outside the walls of my enclosure could be any place in the world. New York. A vacation condo in Florida. A stop-over just off the interstate on an access road in some access town. It all feels the same. Hanoi, Vietnam.

It is 4:45 a.m., and today we drive two and a half hours, away from this large city, through the countryside towards China. I will meet Lily, my daughter, who has been waiting for me for almost a year. I suspect somewhere in her first glance I will see "It's about time you showed up!"

AS I STAND WITH MY BAG in the sheltered alcove of the hotel lobby doors, raindrops splash up at me from the pavement. It is cold for

Hanoi, maybe around fifty degrees. Binh and his driver are bundled up in jackets, gloves and hats when they arrive at 5:30 to pick me up. The heater is cranked up and blowing hard. Within minutes, Binh settles down, hoping to nap during the long drive. For the first hour, there isn't much of interest on the road. Once we leave the city, intersections get farther and farther apart. The road is surprisingly wide, and the rubber of the tires creates a mesmerizing hum on the new, smooth blacktop. This is a main artery for trade with China. Of course it's well-maintained.

Binh sleeps, the radio is silent, and the driver navigates us through the misty darkness, leaving me to my thoughts. The blasting heater lulls me as well, but I don't hope to sleep. Today, life as I know it, life as an independent being, ends. The immensity of this moment isn't swept away by details and appointments and documents now. There is nothing to keep it from spreading and consuming all of my mind. I realize that this is the biggest thing that I have ever done. That includes the day that I got married. And the one that I got divorced as well. I breathe deeply and slowly, trying to balance the feelings of fear and panic, resistance, elation and excitement that accompany impending change and loss of the familiar. *Don't be afraid*, life tells me, *because right now, I am choosing you.*

On this trip, we will turn in my *dossier*. One of the ways that Vietnam differs from other countries is that there is no central countrywide governance of adoptions. Most of the paperwork is handled province by province. And most provinces require that the prospective adoptive parents turn in their paperwork *in person*. This is when they will get the chance to meet their child. The paperwork then takes from four weeks to several months to process, after which time the prospective adoptive parents return to Vietnam to officially adopt the child in what is called a Giving and Receiving Ceremony. This is when custody of the child is turned over to the new parents. The child is now legally adopted as far as Vietnam is concerned. For

Americans, the parents and child then are required to go to the INS in Ho Chi Minh City (formerly Saigon), where U.S. Government officials determine if all of the paperwork is in order, and make sure that the child was not obtained under any shady circumstances, such as mothers being coerced, or offered money, or that the child is who they say she or he is. Unfortunately, unsavory things can and have happened in the world of adoption, including in Vietnam, but where the stakes are high and money is to be made, there are always people who try to take advantage of any situation.

Two trips around the world. The thought of the money and the long flight and the jet lag, and going through it *twice*, was daunting as I first sat making my plans at the dining room table. Yet that is how most people do it. Then again, most adoptive parents are *two*. Two people to organize their paperwork. Two people making the trips. Two people to share in the carrying and lugging and feeding and pushing and bouncing and shopping and picture taking and, and...

Two trips at almost a thousand dollars a pop for airfare. I decided that I would take just one long trip and turn this into a big adventure. I would fly over, turn my paperwork in, meet Lily and spend a few days with her. While the province does whatever it is that they do with my documents for four to six weeks, I would do a grand tour of Southeast Asia. Then I would return to have the Giving and Receiving ceremony. After that, Lily would be all mine, for better and for worse, and we would head back to Norfolk to show her our new home.

EVENTUALLY WE GO THROUGH a toll station, and there is a sign '*tinh Lang Son*'. Lang Son isn't just the name of the main city, but of the entire province as well. My map says we still have about 45 minutes to go. The road has narrowed now to one lane in each direction, and the countryside has changed. We don't pass through any more cities, but occasionally there are clusters of houses on the sides of the road. The terrain has become quite hilly, but in an unusual way. I wouldn't call them mountains, as they aren't that high. But the peaks are abrupt and steep, and pop up and down suddenly from the road level. They are totally covered in foliage, and this morning there is a mist hanging low, partially shrouding their bases, making the tops seem to float above shifting billows of mosquito netting. Anything could be hidden here. Banana trees are scattered along the slopes of the hills, attesting to the tropical climate. If I ever saw the Loch Ness Monster rising out of that mist-shrouded lake, I imagine that this is what it would look like. Only a whole herd of them. These strange hills continue mile after mile, with the road carefully following the valleys in between.

Along the side of the road, the locals are heading to their morning destinations: children walking or riding bikes to school, villagers carting produce, poultry, straw or passengers on bikes or motor bikes, or occasionally a water buffalo. Everything is precariously overloaded. A man rides by with a large pig tied to a stout pole, draped over the back frame of his motorbike. It looks alive to me, and in a very painful position, although it isn't moving.

Eight o'clock. We hit the outskirts of the small city of Lang Son right as scheduled. I don't know if we are going to the government offices to turn in my paperwork first, or if we will go right to the orphanage. Binh answers my unasked question: "The orphanage is down this road."

The SUV makes its way down a dirt road, slooshing through several inches of mud. There are no sidewalks. None of the buildings are over two stories high, and the streets are hung thickly and haphazardly with low, looping cables and electric wires. Another left turn, then we pull through a pair of gates, and are escorted to a stop by a pack of brown, curly-tailed dogs. The building is white-painted cinder block, one story and forms a 'U' around the courtyard. Very utilitarian, nothing soft or pretty.

50

Binh leads the driver and me to a plain front door, and a man with a black beret, a thin mustache and wide grin greets us. This is the orphanage director I am told, and we trade more smiles and handshakes.

Inside, the director offers us a seat on a pair of vinyl couches situated around a low coffee table. On it is a teapot and a half dozen little porcelain cups. He busies himself with boiling some water, then spoons loose tea leaves into the teapot. I look around the room. There is a calendar with a photograph of vibrant pink roses on the top. A framed document hangs over the desk near the back wall. And a long conference table with several stacks of papers on it.

I wonder where the children are? Are they awake and will I get to see rows and rows of babies and children in cribs, or will someone bring Lily to me here? I wonder if they'll make me wait until I turn in the paperwork. I wonder if she will be afraid of me. I wonder everything. I try to keep my face and demeanor relaxed, *calm*, as they chat, as the director pours us some tea into the little cups.

In my belly, I feel as if gravity has doubled on this little spot of the planet. Destiny has brought me to this remote place, half a world away from my home. For this moment, life has chosen me. Western values come face to face with Buddhist philosophy. My mind does not necessarily create my reality. If I entertained any thoughts that I had any input into all of this coming to pass, it was just delusion on my part.

We sip tea. It's awful. It doesn't even taste like tea. We all smile. Nobody says anything. Time struggles by. Finally, "It tastes bad, but it is very good for you." the director offers.

The director and Binh finally rise, and, conversing in Vietnamese, make their way over to the piles of paperwork on the table. Despite the fact that the room is so bare, I haven't noticed until just now that a woman has come in through one of the back doors...holding a baby, a little girl. She has managed to seat herself in one of the chairs without me hearing or seeing her.

She's holding a little girl! They are about twenty feet away. The child is bundled up in several layers of clothing, and there is a cap on her head. It is hard to see her facial details, although I strain my eyes and lean forward a little.

More conversation in Vietnamese. The woman rises and comes closer, she moves toward the men and the conference table. From what I can see of the child's face, she has changed from the photograph, I think, but then the e-mailed image that I had of Baby Thanh, or Lily, looked like it was taken a few months ago. Binh turns to me. "The baby, Baby Thanh, is not available for adoption by you. She has only been in the orphanage for three weeks. The U.S. Embassy has visited the orphanage, and has said that U.S. citizens may only adopt babies who have been in the orphanage for many months."

My gaze leaves his face and travels to the features of the little girl. With Binh's statement, my world wobbles. But right here, in front of me...there is a child... He lifts an open hand towards the child in the woman's arms. "This baby is OK for you to adopt. She has been here since last May. She is Baby Huong." His tone is mat-ter-of-fact. Not the slightest sound of apology.

Through Binh's short speech, the expression remains un-changed on my face. His words penetrate my confusion. This is not the baby, *my* baby. The baby in the photograph that I had copied and placed all over the house, whose face is etched in my memory. The baby that I have fallen in love with from across the world...we have a connection. That baby is somewhere near, but in another room, and there is a child here in front of me, and it's not her...

My mind can't settle on a single thought or feeling for more than the briefest moment. They tumble over each other like tiny pebbles and shells caught in the ocean's surf. No. I will try to adopt the other baby, Baby Thanh, anyway, or I will wait. Or I will adopt this baby and come back for Lily in a few months...hold her for me. I want to see Lily, to see what it feels like to see her, to see if it's her, or if maybe this little girl in this room is her...perhaps *this* is her? *This isn't Lily*!!!

I desperately try to cling to one thought, trying to formulate a response, but it is like trying to grasp those tumbling pebbles in the water with an open hand, the fingers splayed wide. My expectations, my plans that I have created on how this would all turn out begin to dissolve. I force myself to try to let them go. The woman has handed the little girl to the director, who has passed her on to Binh, who then hands her to me. Her body is light and warm and soft. But now she is crying, poor thing, and I have to hand her back to her caretaker. Binh leads me over to the table, and explains that all new paperwork is required, new for *this* child. It will have to be translated back in Hanoi, but I need to sign the papers here for the little girl in the room, La Thi Huong.

I follow him to the table. Do I object, or question, or make a scene? What do I say? There's no one here who can give me advice. It's just me, and what happens now will be irreversible. 'Let go, let go,' is the echoing thought that faintly resounds in my head, and I try to hold on to it.

He takes a moment to assemble the papers that I have to sign. The little girl is four steps away from me, sitting on her caretaker's lap. Thank goodness she has stopped crying. She is still and quiet, almost as if she is holding her breath, waiting for something to happen.

I struggle to open myself to what life is unfolding before me so abruptly. It is as if I have just been asked the final question on a test, and everything hinges on my answer. I believe that life measures us by the choices that we make.

Then I remember that this morning as I was getting ready to leave, I had put a small gray stuffed bear into my jacket pocket, because I thought I might not be able to carry my backpack around with me. I draw the bear out of my pocket, ease it up to near the edge of the table, and make it's head wiggle back and forth.

"Hello! Hello!" I make the bear say. She eyes it with a look somewhere between suspicion and curiosity.

Who is this child? What about Lily? Is this supposed to be Lily, the name I heard in my head months ago? Would making a fuss jeopardize me adopting any child at all? Would that be culturally unacceptable behavior?

I know through the APV list that there are families stuck in Ho Chi Minh City at this moment with children whose documentation is being questioned. I have heard that a child who 'magically' appears to fit the request at the time it is made can be a red flag. Three weeks ago is about the time that I sent the e-mail to Binh saying that I wished to adopt a little girl around one year old. Do I go along with this new development without saying anything? I duck the bear behind the chair, and pop it back out again. "Peek-a-boo!" I say. She smiles. Hide away, pop back out again. "Peek-a-boo!" She smiles. Her caretaker smiles.

Binh calls me back to the documents. Returning to the table, I can't help but wonder if the little girl in the picture that was sent around the world was ever intended to be mine. Perhaps they send a picture of a child that fits the request, and if she's available when the adopting parents show up, fine. If not, well, here's another one…there was a problem. Perhaps they're telling me the truth? I will never ever know, but does it really matter? I wanted a little girl to share my life with. Here is a little girl that the universe is offering up to me. *All you have to do is reach out…*

One page, two page, two places here — I endorse them with the loops that are my signature. I look back at this little girl. I lean over more papers. Binh and the director sort them as I get done with them. They talk to each other some more in Vietnamese. I have brought with me a photo album, of family, of the house that I live in. Some provinces require this as well, although Binh had said it wasn't necessary. I brought it along anyway, and the director pages through it approvingly.

Binh turns back to me. "This is La Thi Huong. Her date of birth is November 11, 2000. You need to remember that when you go to the officials. They will ask you."

I nod and repeat "La Thi Huong." As in most Asian countries, the family name comes first, La, and the given name comes last. The Huong part is difficult to pronounce, but I get fairly close. Thi sounds like 'tea.' It will do, I guess, because Binh and the director start to wrap up the rest of the documents.

I'm finished here I guess, and turn back to this Baby Huong. I look down at her, quietly sitting in her caretaker's lap. A new vision is beginning to condense around me, like the water vapor of a cloud falling together to make a raindrop. She looks up at me. I am still filled with so many conflicting thoughts. I almost reach for the bear, but instead extend both arms out and down, reaching for her. She makes the decision for me. Without hesitation, this little girl, this Baby Huong, her chin and eyes lifted, reaches her arms up to me. She has chosen me.

Her caretaker sucks in a breath in surprise. Even Binh and the director pause in paper shuffling and their conversation to watch as I grasp her under her arms and lift her to me. Baby Huong settles on my hip, one arm resting casually on my shoulder, as if she has always been on that spot. I pick the bear up from the table, and waggle it in front of her. She looks at it, then looks at me, then looks at it. Blinks. Pokes it with her finger. Looks back at me. Not a hint of fear as she looks at this round and hazel-eyed, pale and freckled, red-haired stranger. She has no attachments and expectations to struggle with and release, she is just alive in the world right now and nothing else matters. She is a better Buddhist than I am.

I sit down on one of the couches as the papers are put into Binh's briefcase, then I feel a warmth begin to spread, not in my heart, but across my lap. Baby Huong, it seems, has chosen this moment to baptize me. Disposable diapers are a luxury that orphanages can't afford, and she has been brought in wearing just clothing. Holding her out in front of my body, I stand. A dark patch stands out against the indigo of my jeans, and I wait a moment until my condition is discovered by the others in the room. There is mild panic and startled exclamations. Nobody knows what to do first, but I tell Binh that I have a diaper bag in the SUV. We go out to the courtyard and I pull it out of my larger suitcase. Once inside, I put a diaper on her, as well as a fresh tiny pair of pants. The wet spot on my own pair gradually transitions from warm to cold and clammy.

I'll get the chance, I think, to change them once we're done here and I file the paperwork at the provincial government office. After I check into a hotel in this very dreary, industrial-looking city. Clearly, spending a week or so here, the high points of my day will be the chance to visit this little girl, this Baby Huong...this...Lily?

"The director will come with us," Binh says. "He says you can take the baby with you." I'm puzzled. To the government offices? Do they have to see her as well? Get a footprint or something? Binh clarifies. "I told him that you are staying in Vietnam. He says that you can keep the baby with you until the ceremony."

Apparently I have made a good impression, or perhaps it is because Baby Huong seems quite content to be with me. The director has decided that I can keep this little girl with me as of today. This decision has changed *everything*.

No Cambodia or Thailand. No rugged backpacking trips. This means I will be spending two months traveling in a third-world, communist country with a thirteen-month-old infant. Alone. No, I think, I won't be alone. I will be with Lily. I also don't have the option of pondering this turn of events further. As of now, she is already mine.

AT THE GOVERNMENT OFFICES, I am interviewed by a shivering woman who, like everyone else, is wearing a coat, hat and gloves. There's no heat in this two-story building, but it must be in the upper fifties. I remind myself that Vietnam is roughly equivalent latitude-wise to the Caribbean. Behind her desk, she reminds me of the other government employee who Braille-checked my notarizations, all business and formality. She places a tape recorder between us.

"What is the name of the child that you are adopting?"

"La Thi Huong." I reply, watching the wheels turn around in the window of the little machine.

La Thi Huong is at the moment in my lap and starting to get a little fussy. Binh finds a worker nearby to carry her around and entertain her while I go through this process. More questions. What do I do for a living? Am I capable of supporting this child? Where did you locate the child? Do you agree to send yearly updates to the province about the child's progress?

I am finished in about ten minutes. I hear Baby Huong's cries echoing off the cinderblock walls somewhere down the hall. Binh asks if I have the bottle of warm formula that the woman at the orphanage gave me. It's in the car, I tell him. The car that the driver has left in to go find some breakfast.

The officers who have to finish our paperwork are in a meeting, we are told. It will be perhaps another hour. We sit and wait. Cold tea is in the teapot. A crying little girl is back on my lap (*I think she's just tired, not hungry*). Everyone else is standing or sitting around, waiting, just as cold as the tea.

It crosses my mind that these are my first moments of mommy-hood. I'm still in a bit of shock, she's obviously uncomfortable, and everyone is sitting around without complaining, patiently doing nothing. Such a poor, brave little girl, who has probably spent the past year in one single room, with her surroundings never changing. Today she has been thrown at several new people, taken for a ride in a car, and forced now to do nothing but sit still in this aseptic building. But through all this, there is no mistaking on whose lap she wants to sit.

IT IS NOON, and we are on the highway heading back to Hanoi. Back to Hanoi. No Lang Son hotel, no Baby Thanh. The girl in the photo that I did not get the chance to see is miles behind us at the orphanage, and as each moment passes she gets further and further from our almost-shared future. This baby, here in my lap, has arrived in my life like she has fallen from the sky. I don't think about what I could have or should have said, or whether I did or didn't do the right thing. I feel like I was only present while my life was happening to me. I am along for the ride, and bumpy and crazy though it may be at times, that is just the way that the ride is.

Baby Huong...Lily...sleeps. She is sitting in my arms with her cheek against my warm body. My right arm starts to go numb, but I don't dare move it. I want to let her sleep. So she doesn't have to be awake and try to figure everything out here in a car on the long, boring drive to Hanoi. So we don't run the risk of listening to a child scream in the car for hours and hours.

I wonder who I will tell about this morning's events. What will people think about it? Not that I concern myself too much about impressions, but I don't want it to effect the way people look at the little girl who is right now asleep on my lap. My family and close friends will be supportive, but will others think when they look at her that this isn't the baby I was *supposed* to have? That she was the second choice, second best? Who was really *supposed* to be here? I decide to tell only my family. Until I have had more time to think about it. But the birthdays—the birth-dates are different. I've already told everyone that she will be one year old in January, and now she's showing up at thirteen months...

She sleeps. She is warm and soft, and the expansion of her lungs at each little breath pushes ever so slightly against my own body. She smells of laundry powder and of, hmmmm, cinnamon. This little being is mine to take care of now, to make sure nothing happens to her, to nourish her in all ways. It will be my job twenty-four hours a day for the next year after year after year, whether she is awake or asleep...whether I am awake or asleep. What test did I pass for someone, somewhere to decide that I was deserving of this responsibility?

LILY SLEEPS UNTIL we are half an hour from the hotel. The rest of the way, she curiously looks out at the moving landscape, and we continue our game of peek-a-boo with the bear. This gives me a chance to observe her more closely, now that I'm not rushed or being questioned — or being shocked.

Her skin is as fair as mine, much fairer than the other babies at the hotel, and her eyes are rounder, with very long lashes. She still has two little hats on, a cotton one that ties under her chin, and a little blue and white checkered cap with a bill on top of that. I haven't dared take them off for fear of getting chastised by these freezing Vietnamese. Her eyes are so dark that they look black, with the corneas going almost to the inside and outside corners, but when the sunlight hits them just right, I can see that they are the darkest, darkest of browns, so dark that you can barely make out just a hint of pupil.

She is amazingly relaxed and not fretting the tiniest bit about this drastic, sudden change of surroundings. I am amazed at how in an instant she has accepted me into her life without question. How can she trust me so? Perhaps she has something to teach me.

At the hotel, the ladies at the front desk are excited to see the new arrival. For whatever reason, this particular hotel is popular with several adoption agencies, and at any given time there are half a dozen or so babies coming to and fro. This does nothing to decrease the interest each new one has for the staff. Lily, I tell them her name will be. Her Vietnamese name will be her middle name, Huong.

"Huong!" they repeat in unison, exploding into smiles. Their pronunciation is quite different than mine. I practice with them for a few minutes. With the 'uo' sound, you have to drop your jaw while sliding it forward, and open the back of your throat. Not an easy thing to do for an English speaker. I butcher it. The thought goes through my head that Americans for the rest of her life are going to butcher it.

One of the women tells me "Huong is my name also. Do you know what it means?"

"No...no one has told me yet."

"It means a beautiful smell, like perfume or incense, or the smell from a flower. It is a popular name in Vietnam. Very beautiful."

Lily, Lily, they keep calling her, trying to get her attention with smiles and clucks, but it bothers me a little. I have been calling her Lily as well, but it just doesn't feel...right. Apparently they know that Lily is the name of a flower. There is such importance here on a name meaning something. We try calling her Huong also, but there is no recognition on her part. With many children and probably few caretakers at the orphanage, I wonder how often she was called by her name.

WE RETREAT EVENTUALLY to our, *our*, room, and spend the rest of the day getting to know each other while sitting on the double bed. The first thing I do is take off those hats, and I am surprised by a large clump of hair...black, of course, but so much of it!

I pull out what toys I have brought on the trip with me, a couple more small stuffed animals, some felt rattles and a pacifier that I bought the day before. I take the pacifier out of the bag, and pull apart it's packaging, but she will have nothing to do with it. She is, however, absolutely fascinated by the paper bag and packaging, the way the hard plastic clicks and clunks and buckles when you squeeze it.

"Lily! Lily..." I try again. Lily. It just doesn't sound right, doesn't fit. Somehow it feels attached to the baby in the picture, the baby Thanh who is back in the orphanage in Lang Son. My thoughts stray to the name I have envisioned since I was a teenager, the name before the one in the mirror that my daughter-to-be would have. How about Katherine. After the strong, feisty Ms. Hepburn that I idolized.

"Katherine." I say, as she obliviously tugs with her teeth on the now-spitty paper bag. Katherine. Katherine Huong. I'll try it out for awhile, see how it feels.

I make my first bottle. The first of many, many, I think to myself. I use half hot water from the hotpot, and half from the bottled water in the fridge. The mixture is still a little too warm, and Katherine — Katherine? — is looking a little antsy to get at it. In a hurry I pour some of the bottle contents into one of the tea mugs, put a little more powder in the bottle, screw the top back on, swish it around, take the top off, put a little more cold water in, put the top back on, swish again, feel the plastic bag...it feels better. Katherine's quite displeased with my pathetic, slow efforts, and is starting to get vocal.

We finally settle in though. I sit cross-legged on the bed, back propped against the headboard. She is laying across my lap, head in the crook of my left elbow, and I'm helping her hold the bottle with my right hand. She is happily sucking, swallowing, sucking, swallowing, grasping the sides of the bottle with both hands. Her dark eyes do not move from mine. Nor mine from hers. I am sharply conscious that the energy of her little body is enveloped in the energy of mine, and of the dissolving sense of personal space between us. Of the blurring of the physical boundaries of each of us as separate beings. It is raw, it is mesmerizing, and I suspect that this is just a touch of what I hoped motherhood could be.

Other than the sound of her drinking, there is silence. Gulp, gulp, gulp is the sound that comes not from her throat, but rushes out through her nose with each little exhaled burst of air. I never would have guessed that.

BY THE TIME THE BOTTLE is empty, her eyes have gone from slow-motion blinking to closed completely, her lashes lying on her cheeks like dark feathery tufts of dandelion seed heads. Although her mouth still goes through the motion of sucking, she is asleep.

Carefully I rise from the bed, unfold my legs, place them on the floor, and discover that the left one is asleep. Cradling her body, rocking slightly from side to side, I stand and wait for life to seep back into it. The hotel has brought a crib to the room, complete with sheets, and I place Katherine on her side against a blanket. She immediately rolls onto her stomach, her head turned to the side, her fist in front of her chin.

I crawl on the bed and sit cross-legged again, listening to her breath. The rhythm comes quietly and steadily. It still seems like this can't be true, that I'm not really here, that she's not really here, that us being here together can't really have manifested in my life. But it has. I imagine that I will have a few of these moments before Katherine...yes, I *do* think that it's Katherine...and I feel really like an "us" to me. I get up, pull the camera out of my backpack, take a picture of her, then hold my breath after the flash goes off; I forgot about that. She stirs, pushing with her feet until her head meets resistance on one of the sides of the crib, then settles back down again.

Before I put myself to bed, I finish some of the leftover Indian food cold from the fridge. And I prepare the formula powder in another bottle. All I will have to do when she wakes up in the night is to add water.

I would love to find out more about her, other than her name and her birth-date, but Binh had to take her paperwork with him to have it translated into English. For now she is an absolute mystery to me, as if she really did fall from the sky.

My sleep lasts until about two a.m., when *someone* starts up a crying fit. I'm better at mixing the correct hot and cold water proportions this time. We assume our feeding position, and by the glow of the bathroom light we watch each other in the dimness. Moments follow moments, and her soft breath gradually slows and deepens as she once again falls asleep in my arms.

Chapter opening photograph: Guardians at a tomb, Hue, Vietnam

三

Chapter 4

WITHOUT THE ALARM, I wake before she does. Through the darkness, I faintly hear soft rhythmic breaths. I feel no different, yet everything is different. Between one sunrise and another, all the priorities in my life have shifted down one spot on the list. The well-being of this tiny person now comes before all else. Nothing happens in my life until she is safe and cared for. At the moment she is both of those things, and I rise to turn the hot pot on to boil water for my tea. I add milk and a couple of sugar lumps, and I am able to finish the cup just as movement comes from my right. I watch a little black-haired head rise as she pushes herself upright, looks towards the window where the first light of the sun is starting to come in, then swivels her head around until she sees me sitting on the bed. "Good morning, sweetheart."

She blinks, doesn't smile or cry or make any sound. Just continues to look at me, probably wondering about the odd sounds that are coming out of my mouth. Probably wondering 'who is this person?' Putting the teacup down, I ease over to the edge of the bed and reach into the crib to pick her up. She raises her elbows to let me get a good grip.

In the middle of the bed, she pays no attention to yesterday's refuse that I have tossed onto the sleep-ruffled covers to keep her entertained. Hard plastic packaging, receipts, spoon, paper bag. Katherine is utterly focused on my actions as I mix formula powder, hot water, then cold, in the bottle. Her fists pump up and down in excitement when I turn back to her and climb on the bed. Now she is all smiles and shining eyes. We assume the feeding position, which has so quickly become a routine, and for the first few minutes we become lost falling into each others' eyes. Both of us are still getting used to the idea that neither of us is a dream.

"A week ago" I tell her, "I stood in the middle of your room, looking at your empty crib. The walls are white and they're covered with fairies chasing each other and dancing and carrying flowers." Her gaze never falters, never moves from mine for an instant. Her hands hold onto the sides of the bottle, fingertips gently grasping and releasing. "And there are stars and moons — even a big blue star hanging, and a fairy is hiding on the wall behind it. She's the peek-a-boo fairy. I'll introduce you to her when we get home."

That last night home, standing in the middle of her room, I felt the emptiness there despite the things that filled it. The next time that I stand here, I thought, the life of a little girl will light it up. My intellect told me this was true, but my heart still couldn't wrap itself around what that would feel like.

Now, with her small body resting in my lap, I could feel my heart reaching out to envelop her, like a plant turning towards sunlight. It was falling in love and taking the rest of me with it.

The bottle empties and her trance is broken. She stirs, stretches and rolls from my lap onto the covers, reveling in full-belly happiness. We dress to head out for breakfast at the hotel restaurant. Katherine surprises me with how much she assists by wriggling her arms and legs into her sleeves and pants. These simplest of things that she does without thought I find amazing. She sees no reason to be surprised at the mundanely routine. But for me, each little thing is a totally new departure from my old life, and I am acutely aware of them. Each moment is an opportunity to be mindful, to be utterly absorbed in the present moment.

Where before my Buddhist practice included sitting on a cushion to meditate, reading texts, listening to teachers speak, and practicing being mindful in my daily activities, now *Katherine* will almost exclusively be my daily activity, each and every day. My practice will be being a mommy. Mommy mindfulness. And, as children are naturally mindful, naturally 100% present for every thing that they do, to consciously remind myself to enter into that world with her. That will be her gift of mindfulness to me.

Walking into the dining room with Katherine on my hip, I wave and say hello to the other families who are busy with their own babies. '*Buon Giorno*' from the Italians, a barely accented 'Hello' from the young Swedish couple. No sign of John and Dierdre, but we've got plans to meet in the hotel lobby at nine so they can show me where they bought their stroller.

I order fresh fruit. When it comes, I am surprised by a huge bowl of sliced crimson papaya with a wedge of lime to squeeze over it. There are also some of those tiny yellow fingerling bananas, and two little tangerines. Katherine is awkwardly balanced on my lap as I try to eat, and I watch her as she watches me intently. She shows no interest when I offer her a bite, but is studiously observing me place these colorful items into my mouth. The succulent flesh of the papaya explodes into juice between my teeth. I've never tasted papaya like this before, and I slowly savor the first few bites. She begins to squirm, however, and I am forced to rush through the rest while trying to keep her entertained. She reminds me that my time is no longer just my own.

Soon we go downstairs to meet John and Dierdre in the lobby. Aoefe is seated comfortably in her stroller, and we head off to *Fivimart*, which they tell me has clothing and housewares on the second floor and groceries downstairs, even diapers and formula. Passing through the hotel lobby doors with Katherine in my arms,

I feel the now familiar mist of the air strike the skin of my face. The morning is still cool. She is wearing a long-sleeved shirt and pants, and I have a yellow fleece blanket wrapped around her body. Although I don't know what her weight is, she is an easy enough bundle to carry, less than what two gallons of milk might be.

We have traveled about two blocks when there is a commotion from three women that we are passing on the sidewalk. The conversation between them has shifted to us, and they are frantically signaling, waving their arms, pointing, speaking in words that I have no hope of understanding. One of the women is tapping her leg, and then pointing back to me, to Katherine. I look down. Katherine's pant leg has ridden up and she has approximately two inches of bare leg exposed. Her message is clear: the baby is cold! It is, maybe, sixty degrees out, but I tug the pant leg down smile, nod and we walk on. They seem appeased, but I have the unsettled feeling that my conduct is being scrutinized by everybody. I have been chastised by strangers on the street for negligent care of a baby.

We reach the very Western-style supermarket and attract curious glances from everyone that we pass. Katherine is content riding my hip as we continue upstairs to the second floor. We see several strollers lined up neatly in a row beside a bin overflowing with a rainbow of children's colored plastic sandals. After closer examination, we pick out a collapsible one with a basket underneath, little tray on the front covered with colorful buttons to press, and an awning that extends over top. 356,000 *dong*. I get out my converter cheat-sheet. Less than twenty-five bucks.

With Katherine buckled in, I push her up to the register. The woman behind the counter smiles and leans forward.

"*Em be*," (em-bay) she says. She clucks and jerks her head back a little at the same time. "*Em be*." Cluck-jerk. Cluck-jerk. *Em be*...little girl? Baby? "What is her name?" she asks in English.

"She is Huong," I say, trying to get that jaw-shift, open throat sound just right. "But her American name will be Katherine."

"Katherine," the woman repeats slowly in three distinct syllables, emphasizing the 't' and drawing out a long '-eeen.' "What does that mean?"

What does...I should have known that I'd get asked that question. Who knows? I'm a long way from a baby name book. "It's a family name..." I offer.

"Oooohhhh, yes, a family name. I understand. Kat-er-eeen." She is satisfied.

Downstairs I pick up more supplies: diapers, baby wipes, formula, little soft fabric shoes and several liters of bottled water. My concerns about how easy these items would be to find in this country are put to rest. If I wasn't a health nut, I could even indulge in Coke, Pringles and Oreos. They are all within a few paces of the multitudes of fish sauce bottles, jars of pickles and seaweeds, and packets of noodles and dried fish.

On the way back to the hotel, the strollers roll side by side. I am careful to make sure that the edges of the blanket are tucked in securely and that none of Katherine's skin is exposed. We continue to catch many curious glances, even though it's only a five-block walk. At the final intersection we have to negotiate, we pass a man on a motorbike carrying large plastic containers of orange juice. As he makes his left turn, his head and eyes follow the three Caucasian faces pushing two little Asian ones in strollers down the street. His bike heads straight into the path of another motorbike. Two people and two bikes fall in the collision. About forty gallons of orange juice spill out onto the street. The men rise, lifting their motorbikes from the pavement by the handlebars. We pause long enough to see if they are hurt (they're not), then hurry the rest of the way back to the hotel before any more casualties occur.

AFTER THE GROCERIES ARE STASHED in the hotel room, I roll Katherine through the lobby to begin her first day of sightseeing. The ladies at the front desk stand to lean over the counter, smiling and calling to her.

"Make sure she does not get cold," I am admonished. "She is a *Vietnamese* baby. She is not used to the cold. You must keep her very warm."

Yes, yes, I smile, I nod, assuring them that I will not allow the child to get frostbite. Across the street, the cyclo drivers are at their post, and I walk over to chat for a moment. Katherine eyes Phuc suspiciously, not responding to his grin and enthusiasm. We'll go cyclo later, I tell him, but I'm skeptical myself, wondering about the safety issues of taking her aboard for a ride. With a wave, we head down the street. I decide that a return visit to Uncle Ho is now out of the question with Katherine in tow, so instead we head back towards Old Town and Hoan Kiem Lake. I am keenly aware that everything that we do and see today, every littlest detail, will be new and unfamiliar to her. I don't know if she will respond with fear or curiosity or excitement. Probably a mix of all three.

My own fear of the streets has diminished significantly. Although the curbs can be not very stroller-friendly, I'm getting used to them. The cars and motorbikes, when they see the stroller, now give me much more space. It's like the parting of the Red Sea.

Mostly we just get curious stares from the people we pass, but sometimes, usually by women, we get questioned.

"Vietnam?" they will ask, pointing at Katherine.

"Yes," I say, nodding. "Vietnam."

Ah, they nod to themselves, then point again, and turn to their companions. "Vietnam. Vietnam." It follows us like an echo as we walk down the streets: *Vietnam. Vietnam.*

In Old Town the streets are narrower. So are the sidewalks, and often they are completely blocked with parked motorbikes. So we join right in with the traffic flow. Horns honk, engines buzz and Katherine sits up very straight in her stroller, hands on the tray, fingers resting on the colored buttons. She gazes wide-eyed and silent at the city-dance happening all around her.

One day she is in an orphanage, in an unchanging white cinderblock building. A day later, she is surrounded by this...cacophonous bedlam. She doesn't cry or fuss or show any *fear*. She studies everything she sees. This child, *my daught*er, astounds me with her ability to accept such dramatic change with such calm.

We stop in a few shops where I pick up some gifts and souvenirs. A lotus shaped incense burner, three Buddha statues, as well as three of Quan Am, a robed female incarnation of the Buddha who symbolizes compassion. All are only a few inches tall, as I don't want anything that will be too difficult to carry back. After following a narrow, crooked street lined with gleaming windows full of polished brassware, I pop out unexpectedly near the incense tree on Hang Gai. It's just two blocks to Thuy's silk shop. Although my items won't be ready yet to try on, and she doesn't expect to see me for at least a week, I can't resist stopping by to introduce her to Katherine.

"Oh! You are back! This is the baby! She is very lovely!" She admires Katherine's petite features and long eyelashes, and we chat for a few minutes. When she asks how long we will stay in Hanoi waiting for the adoption to be final, I tell her that it takes six weeks, and that I plan to see a little more of the country—with Katherine.

"I will hold your things for you then, until you are ready to take them with you," she says as we wave goodbye. I ease the stroller out the door, between some motorbikes, and back onto the busy sidewalk.

At all of the stores, with all of their faces, Katherine glances often at me, making sure that I remain within reach. Out of the stroller, she clings to me, denying all effort by anyone else who tries to hold her for me. But she is friendly, smiling much, and charmed easily by these people who seem to have such open affection for little ones.

At Hoan Kiem Lake, the vendors still flock to me, only this time instead of "Missy! Missy!" their cry is "Madam! Madam!" I really *have* graduated to motherhood. "For the baby!" they tell me, now holding out tiny-sized t-shirts.

Katherine is my ambassador. She is an invitation who entices anyone and everyone to strike up a conversation with this Western woman. The deeper I get into tourist territory, the more English the Vietnamese tend to speak, and the bolder they become. Near the bridge to the pagoda, some teenagers come up and squat down in front of the stroller. "Vietnam?" they ask. Cluck, cluck, cluck, boys and girls alike. *"Em be!"*

Katherine looks out at them from her stroller, not smiling, but not afraid. Just watching. Within moments, a group of over a dozen has formed, and they crowd around us, pressing closer before I have a chance to retreat. She finally hits her tolerance limit. I see a worried look cross her face, and before I can push through the crowd, she is wailing. "Bye bye!" I say as I shove through. They part, she cries, I hurry. At the next bench there is no one near, and I sit down to talk and comfort her.

"You're OK, sweetie, you're OK," I say, wiping the tears from the corners of her eyes with the edge of the blanket. She has already stopped crying, and I make a mental note to be a more prepared next time.

We round the bend of the lake. There is a two-story restaurant and café there with outdoor seating. They sell pastries, café and tea, sandwiches and…ice cream. I get a scoop of my favorite, mint chocolate chip, in a cup with a plastic spoon. We sit by the lake at a little iron table, and I put just a bit on the end of the spoon and hold it out to her. She looks at it. I move it a little closer. She moves her head back to get away from the spoon, eyeing it cautiously. I put a bit on my finger, and wipe a smudge of ice cream on her lips. She is furious, thrashing her legs, glaring at me accusingly, trying to dislodge the cold substance from her lips with her fingertips. She doesn't completely succeed and finally licks her lips. There is a pause as I watch her mentally processing the feedback from her taste-buds. Her expression metamorphoses from pinched and angry to excited. Her arm shoots up and a very demanding index finger jabs towards the spoon that is still hovering in my hand.

"You want more, I take it?" I ask her.

"Mmm" she grunts, pressing her lips together. Her whole arm is waggling as she makes sure that I can see the pointing. She scoots from side to side in her stroller, popping up a little with each "Mmm!"

As she allows the spoon to pass between her lips this time, her expression is rapturous, her limbs contract and quiver. She tastes it with her whole body. First ice cream. What a reaction. It is probably the closest that I will ever get to tasting ice cream for the first time again, watching this little girl, my daughter, do it. The trick is, I guess, to keep your eyes open and pay attention, otherwise you will miss these moments. This is 'mommy mindfulness.' I am completely absorbed in the present moment, enjoying ice cream for the first time with Katherine, and nothing else in the world matters right now. All there is is right here and right now.

By the time evening rolls around, I have covered I don't know how many miles, and Katherine never fell asleep for one little bit of it. When I settle on the bed with Katherine on my lap for her dinner bottle, we easily find our comfortable, now-familiar position. She gulps away and keeps her eyes fixed on mine. Tonight though, she reaches out with one hand and explores my face with her fingers. Poke, poke to my cheeks and eyelids, squeeze to my nose. Lips, teeth, skin. Hey, hey — nostrils! I let her explore my features, this face that she is getting used to.

In turn, I run my own fingers over and down her arms and her legs, feeling the tiny toes inside her socks, running my fingertip along the valley on the bottom of her foot that separates the sole from the digits. So fragile! She responds by curling them around my finger. I gently roll each little toe between my thumb and index finger. They feel like soft little beans inside the skin of a wrinkled pod.

After her bottle, I go to the crib to lay Katherine down to sleep. The honeymoon is over. She lets out a wail that escalates to hysterical screaming that no amount of carrying, bouncing, shushing or patting will silence. After forty-five minutes of bouncing, patting and humming my way around the room I feel as if an evil twin has replaced my angel-child. Nothing I can think of placates her, and I have to wait for her to eventually cry herself to sleep. All sense of calm or peace has been driven far, far from my consciousness. Is she hurting? Was she hungry? Was she scared? Is she teething? Have a bellyache? Who knows? Shouldn't I have magically acquired the intuition to know these sorts of things when they placed her in my arms? Do I really think that I can take care of this little being after all?

I sag onto the edge of the bed and try to fill my mind with all of the wonderful moments we shared during the day. I close my eyes and draw deep breaths of air slowly into my lungs. After a while, this helps, and I hear little snores coming from the direction of the crib. When I walk over to look in, I see an angelic pink-cheeked cherub peacefully laying on her belly like a little frog. The thought of SIDS crosses my mind, that perhaps I should turn her onto her side or back, but I can't bring myself to possibly awaken her. Chances are she's slept like this for the past year of her life.

I call John and Deidre's room to see if one of them can sit with her while I pop off a quick e-mail home. John doesn't half believe my screaming banshee story. They have only seen the inquisitive, charming little angel-Katherine. Deidre comes in to sit while John bounces their own little crying daughter in the courtyard.

No one at home expects to hear from me for at least a week. I'm also not quite sure what to mention about the turn of events in the orphanage director's office. How can I possibly communicate all of that in an e-mail? And how much of it do I want to share right now or ever? My whole being has accepted that *this* child is the child who was destined to be placed on my lap, *this* child is the little girl with whom I will share the adventure of my life. But inevitably I know some people will think or say: "She wasn't the baby from the photograph? Do you think you were intentionally mislead?" or "Do you wonder about that other little girl?" I need to ponder this a little more, and I decide to skirt the issue for the moment, perhaps just sending more details off to close family later.

Subj: We're in Hanoi!
Date: 12/14/01 8:51:29 PM
From: Efitz
To: Vietnam Group
Sent from the Internet (Details)

Hi everyone! Me again already!

News brief: Apparently the orphanage director took a shine to me, and Lily did too right away, so they let me take her back to Hanoi with me. So here we are! Also, now she seems like a Katherine. Identity crisis aside, Katherine is a WONDERFUL baby! There was a miscalculation with the paperwork, and her birthday isn't in January like I thought, but November 11th, so I have a little thirteen-month old Scorpio on my hands.

Very inquisitive and curious and mild-mannered. We were all over town today in a stroller, and she was a big hit with everyone we passed—even inadvertently caused a scooter accident when a guy who watching us go by instead of where he was going and who was hauling orange juice collided with another motorbike. No casualties except for the OJ thankfully!

Anyway, going to run. Just wanted to pass the happy news on!

Love, Ellen

PS- Although I had only changed one diaper in my entire life before this trip, I already have the 60-second diaper change down pat!

BACK IN THE ROOM, a long night is just beginning. Katherine is restless, and she wakes up and cries every few hours. Patting is a no-no, I figure out. She much prefers either rubbing on her back, or better yet, for me to gently roll the crib back and forth while she lays in it. After the third waking session, I try sleeping diagonally across the bed, with my arm dangling off the side, holding onto one of the crib rails and push, pull, push, pull. Click click click, pause, click click click, as the wheels rolls over the cracks between the tiles. After awhile, I could almost fall asleep and keep the rhythm going while unconscious. Click click click...click click click...

BINH HEARD BACK FROM THE ORPHANAGE director today. He says that it is OK to take Katherine to Hue, in central Vietnam. I just need to make sure that I have all of Katherine's paperwork with me when I travel, so he will be dropping it off at the hotel this afternoon.

Tomorrow my friend Allen will be in Hanoi. He leads the meditation group that I belong to back in Norfolk. The group's practice is based on the Buddhist tradition and the teachings of Thich Nhat Hanh. Allen is in Vietnam to oversee some of the social projects that our group initiated and supports in the city of Hue, primarily a school for children with disabilities. It is because of the connections of our group that I began an independent adoption instead of going through an agency.

In Hue, Katherine and I will be able to relax among friends instead of frittering away six weeks in a hotel room. We'll be able to see the school, maybe help out a little, and meet the Buddhist nuns who run it.

I will make my travel arrangements after I see what Allen's plans are. So Katherine and I still have another two days to explore

Hanoi, and, more importantly, explore each other. I'm getting used to the idea that I can't pee by myself. The first time that I tried to go to the bathroom, she threw a screaming fit as soon as I left her sight. I had to pick her up and bring her into the bathroom with me. And this morning when I rolled the stroller out onto the patio to sweep the crumbs out, she had the same reaction…she thought that I was leaving without her. The fact that she has without question accepted that she and I are a pair now, so quickly, is humbling and scary and intense. Not that she has much of a choice at this age, but the unconditional trust she has placed in me is such a responsibility. I don't ever want to do anything that will break that trust, or disappoint her. Several times when an Asian woman has tried to hold her or comfort her when she was fussy, thinking that a more familiar-looking face would calm her, Katherine only reached out to come back to me. I am hers and she is mine because *she* says so, not because some official papers do.

She is an angel. She is magnetic. She is ecstatic. She is joyous. She is funny. This morning I'm getting a few things organized to make packing easier tomorrow. I'm facing away from the bed where she is playing with her expensive toys (wrappers, receipts and plastic cups), when all of a sudden it is very quiet, and I turn around to see what's up. There she is, sitting in the middle of the bed, with a Williams-Sonoma dishtowel draped over her head. She sits motionless, head bowed, waiting…waiting for me to see her and lift it and say peek-a-boo and laugh. She has done this to be funny and make me laugh! She has been on this planet for only a little over a year, and she has figured out how to do something to entertain someone else. It amazes me. I lift it from her face, and she explodes with giggles and smiles and shrieks. Her eyes scrunch up, and she falls over, she can hardly stand it. So this is what I've been missing out on! Moments later, we are lying on the bed, side by side, facing each other, now serious. She reaches out to touch my face, then my open hand resting palm-up on the comforter. With her tiny index finger, she touches the lines that criss-cross the surface. Life line, heart line, I think to myself...where is the line where you come in, little girl? Then she tries to grasp one between her thumb and finger, tries to lift it off my palm as if it were a hair or filament, and is surprised to see that it's a part of me.

An hour later, she is 'cruising', trying to walk while hanging onto the bed, a chair, the TV stand. As she pauses at the stand, she turns to see if I am watching. I am just about to acknowledge her triumphs, when her foot slips, and she spins, twisting, falling to the floor. The look on her face is surprised fear, and I can't move fast enough to stop it. She doesn't hit anything very hard, so she's not hurt. I scoop her up just as she finishes that first big in-breath to let out a wail. How she screams and squeezes me. Save me, help me! She buries her face in my neck and is grasping my shirt with her hands, while her feet push up against my legs. It is almost as if she is trying to climb inside of me, she can't get close enough to me. I hug and hold her and hum. All I can do is be here, and let her know that I am here. In the space of an hour I have experienced her ecstasy and her despair. Both make me love her more, and I think of how I will spend many years seeing her continue to experience both, sharing them with her, and everything in between.

After breakfast we head out on our walk in the opposite direction from the Old Town. I am getting tired of fighting off the hawkers. I have bought my t-shirts, mini straw hats and postcards. My chant as I shake my head no is "I have, I have, I have...no, sorry, I have."

Our first stop is a clinic not too far from the hotel, where there are supposed to be English-speaking doctors. I want to make sure that nothing harmful is causing her crying at night. She weighs in at 15 pounds and gets a clean bill of health. The crying is probably just due to some teething.

We continue to the area of town called the French Quarter. When Vietnam was a French colony, this area was built up with Parisian-style homes, even an opera house, hence the name French Quarter.

We pass several women with baskets and buckets of flowers set out around them on the sidewalk. They smile. One of them breaks off a small purple flower and holds it out to Katherine. Katherine looks, but doesn't reach out to take. "Vietnam?" the older woman asks, and I nod and say "yes, Vietnam."

She looks at me questioningly, points at Katherine and holds up her index finger. This has happened a few times over the past three days, and I nod, hold up my own index finger and say "Yes, she's one year old." The woman points to Katherine, then to me, then picks up the blanket on Katherine's lap as if to peek under it, and points back towards me...below the waist. Oh! I laugh, then nod again. "Yes, she's a girl!" Now I know what she had been holding her finger up about! Finger...boy. Was the baby a boy! They laugh as well, we smile and nod and have a regular girl moment right there on the sidewalk, although we don't share a spoken language.

We wave goodbye. "Vietnam, Vietnam" is the chorus that fades away behind us. Katherine is now holding her purple flower, but not for long. Today's project, beginning at breakfast, is to test the law of gravity. It hits the sidewalk, and she pulls herself forward to look down, pointing with her index finger at it lying there. Yep, Katherine, gravity is still working this afternoon.

We pass 'barber shops,' which are just spots along the sidewalk where someone has set up a stool, hangs a mirror on a wall or fence, and cuts hair right out on the street. There is also a dentist's office with the chair right in the front, full-length window, letting passers-by get a show of the current treatment being rendered.

We find a shop called Gourmet Hanoi, and inside they are selling real French cheeses and wine, sausages and pates, and *terrines*. The place smells like feet, so I know it's authentic. The young girls working there don't speak any English, but they do speak French.

They ask if Katherine's father is Vietnamese. Um, yes, he is, but so is her mother. Oh! They are surprised. They tell me they thought she was my child because she is fairer than most Vietnamese babies, with a thin face like mine, and has rounder eyes. And how thick her hair is! *"Une belle petite enfant,"* they say. I can't agree with them more.

Back at the hotel, the front desk has Katherine's papers waiting for me in a brown envelope. I take them back to the room to read after she goes to sleep. She consumes a bottle in utter peace and tranquility as we bask in each others' presence, she frazzles my nerves with a 45 minute cry, then she's out.

I flip up the metal tabs on the envelope and draw out about a dozen documents. The top one is her birth certificate. Although she was born November 11th of 2000, the birth certificate was filed on January 9th, 2001. There is a picture of her in the upper right hand corner; that would put her at almost two months of age. She is crying, wearing a well-worn, faded, yellow sweatsuit and lying on a red floral blanket. She looks lost and afraid. It makes me long to have been there to protect her then.

There are also the official documents from the province and the orphanage. I am surprised to find that she spent the first six months of her life with her birthmother, and was then relinquished to the orphanage in May of this year. The relinquishment papers are there, a statement why her mother can't keep her. Then I find another relinquishment paper...from her birthfather. They are Nung, one of the minority groups in Vietnam that is ethnically Chinese. They are married. There are photos of them both. I see immediately that she favors her birthfather the most. The eyebrows, the oval shaped face, the fair skin tone. Their written stories echo each other: they have many other children and live in such poverty that they are barely able to care for them, let alone one more little girl. After discussing it with their family, they have decided to relinquish her to the orphanage. In their letter they ask the province to help find a good home for her. They were both born in 1972, both 28 years old when their Huong was born.

Their facial muscles hold no expression. There is no smile, no frown, no worry crinkles between the eyebrows. It is only in the piercing look of her mother's dark eyes that I see any hint of the agony she must be suffering by giving up this little girl in hopes of a better life for her.

I glance over at the crib. As usual, Katherine has pushed herself up until the top of her head rests against one of the sides. She is so tiny that she comfortably lays across it lengthwise. One leg is pushed through the bars, and a blue-socked foot dangles loosely in the air. My stomach contracts looking at that foot, and I feel a surge of tenderness. It had not occurred to me that I might possibly learn this much information about her history, about her birthparents. So often I have heard about abandoned babies who never have any links to where they are from and what their stories are. Especially in China, where they have the one-child rule. And in Vietnam, as in so many countries, there is great social stigma against unwed mothers. But the fact that poverty is the sole reason for giving up a child is distressing — and I am ashamed that my ignorance and blindness comes from living in such an affluent country.

Knowing that Katherine has an identified birthfamily brings up more questions for me. Down the road, tracing them will take little more effort than pulling out a map and finding their village. Will she want to find and visit her birthmother at some point? If she does, I will help her.

What a different life Katherine will lead from the brothers and sisters that she is leaving behind! School. Shoes. Warm food, guaranteed, every day. Then beyond the basics: music lessons, art and many other experiences that we take for granted. I'm not rolling in dough, but even the simplest life home in the States would be considered luxurious in Vietnam.

I look again at her birthmother's picture. After giving birth to this little girl, and caring for her for six months, how wrenching it must have been to give her up. How much sadness she must have endured, must continue to endure. She doesn't even know that Huong, Katherine, will end up in America. And that she will be loved.

THE NEXT EVENING, we meet up with Allen. Actually, he hops a ride on a motorbike from Old Town and comes to our hotel. We walk over to Café Pho, as it is pretty there at night, strung with twinkling white Christmas lights. Katherine flirts with the waiter. He brings her a peeled apple, which she sucks on for a few minutes, then tests gravity again. Allen tries to interest her in playing copycat, clapping hands, putting her hands on her head, banging on the tray. He is at work. He is a professor at Old Dominion University in Special Education. That's how we ended up being involved in the school project in Hue. He can't help himself but to evaluate her responses and activity.

"Allen! Hello!" I say, trying to get his attention. "When are you flying to Hue?"

"Look at that!" he says excitedly. "She put her hands on her head, right after seeing me do it! Look how quick she is!"

I could easily let him go on about how intelligent my daughter is.

"Allen, you're used to working with developmentally disabled and profoundly retarded children. Of course she's quick!"

"I guess you're right," he says, and continues to play his little games with her. I think that she is entranced with his looks: she has never seen a bearded person with glasses before.

I finally get out of him that he'll be leaving for Hue in two days. First he has some meetings to attend in Hanoi as well as get some supplies for the school. I tell him that the noise and exhaust fumes in Hanoi are giving me headaches and making me feel queasy. And just about all men smoke. Everywhere. Especially the Italians in the lobby of the hotel. I am not used to all this pollution. I want to leave for Hue Sunday, which would beat him down there by two days.

"Don't worry," I tell him. "We'll wing it until you get there. We'll be fine."

Chapter opening photograph: Katherine Huong on our first night together

四

Chapter 5

WE FLY TO HUE SUNDAY afternoon on Vietnam Airlines. I buckle into the seat with Katherine sitting on my lap. There is a loud click as the plane's intercom system is turned on:

"This is the captain speaking…" a male voice, unquestioningly American, begins, and the non-accent of his voice puts me at ease. The flight will be a little more than an hour, he tells us "The temperature in Hue is 78 degrees. It is raining."

I wonder what the city of Hue will be like, and what the countryside will look like from the window of the airplane. Hue was the home of the last Vietnamese emperors, the Nguyen Dynasty, and it was the capital of Vietnam for much of the past 200 years. It was also the site of the Tet Offensive in 1968, one of the worst battles of the American War. Thousands of people were killed. North Vietnamese. South Vietnamese. Civilians. Americans.

It is the closest large city to the 17th Parallel, the invisible line that was drawn to separate the north and the south that ultimately failed in keeping the two halves as a divided country. For years this dividing line and the Demilitarized Zone surrounding it was defoliated, carpet-bombed and napalmed. I wonder if I will see the inevitable scars on the land and the shells of destroyed structures, or will elapsed time be able to hide the memory of what happened here?

I'm a little nervous about this being Katherine's first flight, but I have come prepared. A warm bottle is wrapped up and hidden in the diaper bag as I wait for the crucial moment of takeoff. When it comes, I time it perfectly. Warm bottle, happy baby, no crying. I had envisioned invisible daggers being thrown at the back of my head as the mother of the baby who screams for the whole hour and a half flight.

Although most of the people boarding the plane are Asian, it turns out that I share my aisle with an American family. The two parents are accompanied by their less-than-enthusiastic pre-teen son and daughter. Both have their faces buried in books. As the plane cruises towards Hue, Katherine plays peek-a-boo with several of the passengers behind us. The American woman and I compare what our guidebooks say about hotels. Neither of us has made reservations yet.

Following a list of the major expensive hotels is a description of some tourist villas, converted colonial houses along Ly Thuong Kiet. Street names in Vietnam never actually end with 'road' or 'street.' Most are simply the names of historical figures, like kings, generals or heroes — and more recently, Communist Party leaders. With thousands of years of history of invasions, occupations and liberations, there is no shortage of names from which to choose.

At $10 a night, these guest villas sound affordable and full of atmosphere. The family will be taking a taxi into town and would share with me, but with four people and luggage, they will fill it up. I'll go on my own but we make tentative plans to meet there.

Once we land, I find that there is a tourist bus that takes passengers to their hotels. I buy our bus ticket after picking up the luggage from the carousel. The Army Guesthouse in Hanoi has thankfully allowed me to store my extra things there that I don't need, as well as the gifts that I'll be bringing home. I'll be picking it all up when I go back to Hanoi for the official adoption ceremony.

It is warmer in Hue than it was in Hanoi. Ho Chi Minh City will be even more so. Vietnam is a very slender, but very long country. The distance between Hanoi and HCMC is about the same distance between Washington, D.C. and Jacksonville, Florida, but in the south the climate is tropical like the Caribbean. This made it a challenge when I was packing for the trip. I had to bring clothes for different climates, as well as several sizes of baby clothes and diapers, since I didn't know what size this little girl would be. Katherine ended up fitting into the smallest of everything that I had brought.

I juggle one stroller, one small backpack, a diaper bag and my trusty rolling backpack-suitcase. And one baby. It is raining, and the droplets are warm and soft. The other passengers, tourists all, help me load my things onto the shuttle bus. There are European and Australian backpackers, and another American family. It is a few miles into Hue from the airport, and everything about the view from the window is refreshingly not like Hanoi. There are less cars and trucks, more bicycles and decidedly less noise. We first make a few stops at the big hotels, the Century, L'Indochine, then smaller ones like the Binh Minh. Eventually, we pull up at the address that I gave them from my book. The driver takes a second look at the address. It must not be one of his regular stops.

We are at the end of a driveway, and the few remaining passengers help me with my bags, passing them overhead to the front of the bus. As the bus disappears down the street, we start up the driveway. Katherine is in her stroller, I wear my backpack and the diaper bag, and I pull the rolling bag behind me. A man comes out onto the porch of the L-shaped, single-story complex and tells me that they are closed for renovations.

I stop and take a deep breath as his comment sinks in. Raindrops continue to sprinkle my head and shoulders, the bags, and the awning of Katherine's stroller. I pull out my map long enough to see the general direction of some of the other hotels, then fold it away before it too gets soggy. The nearest one is at least five blocks away. There is no sign of my American friends. I start walking. I make it as far as two driveways down, when another man comes walking out from a different large house.

"Where do you go?" he asks, and I tell him about my dilemma with the tourist villas. "We have rooms here, and nobody is staying right now, so you can have any one you want."

The rain falls, and I pause for barely a moment before following him up the path. It turns out that this is also one of those left-behind French colonial homes that is now an informal guest house. There is a wide porch in front with tall white columns rising as high as the roof. Inside, there is a kitchen, as well as several large guest rooms. Out back, there is a smaller building where Trung, my host, stays. Trung speaks pretty good English, and he proudly shows me a guest book where previous lodgers have left their compliments and anecdotes. There are business cards too, from California, New York, Chicago, Florida, London. By now, a small crowd has gathered: Trung's sister and mother, and six children. Some are his sister's, and some are visiting. No one else speaks English, but they smile a lot, and are, as usual, quite fascinated with Katherine. They help me settle in, carrying my bags and making sure that I have boiling water in a thermos. A tea pot and cups are set out on a table on the porch, and a few minutes later, Katherine and I are sitting out with the family, watching the rain sprinkle the ground.

He tells me that his family runs this place, and that his cousin is a medical doctor in California. I tell him about adopting Katherine and about my Norfolk group's involvement with the school in Hue. He says that he's never heard of our school, but then again, I couldn't tell him exactly where it was. Then I ask if he knows of Thich Nhat Hanh, the Buddhist monk.

"Yes," he says, he has. "He is famous."

"I would like to go to see the pagoda, his root temple." I tell him. It is here in Hue.

"Yes, I know it. I can take you there. We can go on the motor-bike."

"Maybe later…I have to take care of Katherine…" I say.

"She can stay here with my sister. She will take care of her."

Katherine is already sitting on sister's lap, and the other children hold her attention. I am very tempted. Back home in the States, I would never leave Katherine with someone that I didn't know, but somehow here it is different. Vietnam is such a child-oriented culture. Grandparents spoil their grandchildren, like everywhere. But here children care for other children. Even teenage boys feel comfortable cooing and interacting with little ones. I haven't had a break for a week. I am sleep deprived. As wonderful as Katherine has been through everything, I am tired from being 'on-duty' every moment for the past week. The thought of a few minutes on my own sounds delicious.

"When do you want to go?" I ask, watching the water shudder on the surface of puddles as the raindrops continue to fall from the sky.

"Now." Trung says, rising. He says a few words to his sister, and disappears around the side of the house. A moment later he appears leading a motorbike by the handlebars, and he hops on the seat. "Go," his sister nods to me, and seeing that Katherine is content, I step out from the shelter of the porch and climb on the bike behind him. The back tire skitters a bit on the gravel and mud, then we bounce down over the curb and into the street. I search for a moment for a place to hang onto, and finally find the lip under the sides of the seat. The rain feels good on my face. I take a deep breath. I feel light.

He takes me down the road about five traffic lights, turns left and goes over some train tracks. Immediately past these he turns left again, but not onto a street. It is more like an extra-wide side-walk that parallels the tracks. We pass a few courtyards to some homes, then an area overgrown with foliage. Soon we reach a stone-paved wide entranceway with a pillared archway at the top.

This is it, he indicates, but I should walk up, as the bike will not have good traction on the slope. My feet slip a lot, and I use a hand on the short wall at the edge to help keep my balance. Trung passes by me, rubber sliding on moss and stone. Both of his feet are stuck out to the sides to steady his ascent, and he disappears after passing beneath the arches. Following behind him, I enter a heavily-treed garden, the highest branches stretching far overhead. There are two small stone kiosks that hold Buddha statues on either side, each with a peaked roof supported by pillars extending out in front. It is very quiet, the main sound being the raindrops falling on the fat green leaves of the tropical foliage.

Trung appears after leaving the bike somewhere out of sight, and motions me toward a larger building further to the back. It is an open-air temple. Not the main hall, but it has various statues and decorative pieces. We meet a brown-robed monk there. His head is, like all monks, and Buddhist nuns for that matter, shaved. He smiles and places his palms together, bowing his upper body forward. We do the same to him. I feel quite comfortable returning this gesture, having practiced it so often in Plum Village. It is an acknowledgement of the Buddha-nature in ourselves as well as others. The part inside each of us that we can touch to realize our true selves and the true nature of all that is.

The monk leads us to the main temple. There is a large golden statue of the Buddha, as well as Quan Am and other *Boddhisattvas*, sort of Buddhist saints. There are also embroidered silk alter hangings, carved wooden tables and alters draped with elaborate cloth, and on the other side of the room, a long wooden dining table with benches, enough to sit a couple dozen monks. There is the pungent tingle of incense burning (Huong! I think with a smile). Always incense burning.

Our monk doesn't speak any English, but leads us through the hall with calm grace, pausing in front of the primary altars so I can admire them. There are only a few monks left at this pagoda now,

Trung tells me. Not as many as a few years ago. I place a donation, a U.S. five dollar bill folded in quarters, into a wooden box. Our monk strikes a brass bowl with a padded stick, and the tone resonates off of the walls of the hall. I smile and am happy that I have gotten a chance to visit this place where my teacher has not been able to return for over thirty years. During the war, and all the way up until today, the Buddhist nuns and monks have been the 'rabble-rousers,' not hesitating to make public political statements against the government. Not the sort of thing that goes over with a Communist administration, and they are watched closely. Thich Nhat Hanh was at the forefront, speaking out for an end to fighting in the sixties, and was even nominated for a Nobel Peace Prize by Dr. Martin Luther King, Jr. But his teachings have not been 'officially' welcome here since then.

As Trung leads the way out, I am surprised to feel a tiny bit disappointed. Somehow I thought that there would be more to it, or that I would see some connection to my teacher. Perhaps if there had been someone to talk to, to share my feelings with about being here, it would have made a difference. Now I feel ashamed at my disappointment, at how I have obviously placed my own expectations on what I thought this experience would be.

Trung wheels the motorbike down the slope before we climb back on. Seated behind him, I thank him for bringing me here before he gains enough speed to make conversation impossible due to the wind. We are back at the house before 45 minutes have passed, and Katherine is not only comfortable, she is asleep in her stroller in my room. One of the girls, I guess about twelve years old, is sitting in a chair next to her, quietly reading a book. Her long hair is pulled back in a ponytail, the length flowing along the path of her spine between her shoulder-blades.

"We will go eat," Trung says. He says a few words to the girl, and she turns back to her book. I follow in his steps out the front door towards the street.

The rain has, thankfully, stopped, and when we reach the sidewalk, we turn left. About thirty feet away, a woman has set up a cart from which she sells chicken and soup. There are plastic chairs and tables sitting out on the sidewalk in front of the cart, but they are kiddie-sized. About the height that you would see in a kindergarten class. We take a seat, and she brings out two large steaming bowls of chicken soup with rice in it, two small plates, each with a whole chicken leg on it, and a condiment tray with a pile of salt, lime wedges and chopped cilantro. She leaves and returns again with two locally brewed 'Hue' beers in oversized bottles. Our dishes and bottles barely fit on the surface of the tiny table, and we sit roadside, literally one foot from the curb, eating wonderful soup with our elbows resting on our knees. The lime wedges are for squeezing into the soup. Trung chucks his into the gutter after squeezing the juice free from the rind.

I turn to the chicken leg last and it is…horrible. It is tough and sinewy, and my first thought is that it was a shame that the animal died to be such a poor dinner. I can barely whittle away at the leg, and the spaces between my teeth fill with chicken flesh fibers. I have to leave the leg unfinished. I don't want to be wasteful, but I can't get any further with it. Trung, meanwhile, has stripped his of joint cartilage and everything. I smile thinking that this thrifty woman will hardly let mine go to waste. It will probably end up in tomorrow's pot.

WHEN WE ARE DONE EATING, Trung passes me a plate with toothpicks on it, and tells me that the bill is 47,000 *dong*…I guess I'm buying. Still not bad for a little over three bucks.

When I return to the house, Trung's sister and all the children are on the porch. Katherine is in his sister's arms and is excitedly beating her over the head with her fists in play. I am horrified. She has *never* done that with me! The sister, however, ducks and laughs, ducks and laughs. *Don't even think it, little one,* passes through my mind as I reach for her. She doesn't. Instead, her arms wrap around my neck and she holds tight as if to make sure that I don't slip away from her again.

The clouds continue to hold back for now, and we have perhaps an hour and a half of light left to do some exploring. We walk towards the river. Hue is bisected by the Perfume (Huong!) River. The Southeast side, where we are, is where most of the hotels, restaurants and businesses are. The Northwest side is where the Citadel is, a stone-walled fortress accessed through formidable gates. The Forbidden City is enclosed inside the protective embrace of the Citadel, and is where the last emperors of Vietnam resided.

We pass some of the fancier hotels and some outdoor restaurants, and pause at one of the cafés for some cold coconut juice from a can. Katherine has learned to share with me by waiting for me to suction some juice up in a straw, then drinking it out of the bottom when I hold it for her, releasing my finger. A time consuming process, but it usually amuses the people occupying the tables around us. Walking again, we cross Le Loi, the wide boulevard that runs along the banks of the Perfume River.

At the next intersection, we roll up the ramp of Trang Tien bridge. It spans the river and has a section in the middle for the motorbikes, bicycles and cyclos. No cars allowed. There are walkways along the sides for pedestrians. We leisurely stroll across, only to turn around at the far end to try to beat the sunset home. Halfway back across, we meet some teenagers, and one of the girls remarks how pretty Katherine is, in excellent English. I thank her, and comment on how lovely the river view is.

"Your English is quite good," I add, "better than most people that I have spoken to here."

She giggles. "I'm Australian!" Her friends join in on the laughter. The joke's on me and I laugh, too.

They are on a school trip, and are working their way up the country from South to North. All in the group are Vietnamese in heritage, however, and this is their first chance to see the country of their parents.

Dusk is falling, and the neon sign of the Hue brewery on the Northeast bank begins to glow intensely red. One of the boys points straight down from the bridge into the water. "Look!"

We all get close to the rail and lean over. There are red and green candles bobbing on the surface of the river, first just a scattered few, then larger and larger bunches. Behind us, upstream, there are wooden boats to the west of the bridge, mostly carrying tourists. In the old days on special occasions, candles were traditionally set afloat on the river for good luck. Now the tourist boats make it a regular occurrence. Dusk deepens, and the clusters slowly drift, red and green, twinkling their way downstream. Past the bright lights of the brewery, past the last few river bank hotels, and out into the darkness on their way to the South China Sea.

By the time we get back to the guesthouse it is dark. There is no sign of Trung's sister, or the little ones. Leaving the stroller on the front porch, I go to our room and fix a bottle for Katherine from the water in the thermos. She seems a little uneasy here, and is fussy and even a little clingy. The room has gotten chilly and clammy with the evening, and I dress her in an extra layer for warmth.

The ceilings in the room are very high and the plaster walls are bare, so noises and voices send out an odd resonance. I feel uneasy as well, then I realize that I got the same feeling in the director's office at the orphanage. Cold, non-cozy and bare. Perhaps she feels it, too. There isn't a crib here, so we will share the bed. This poses a problem, as she is so used to sleeping in an enclosed crib that she has developed that habit of scooting herself up until her head hits something. She's likely to push herself right off the bed! This bed is on a solid platform, so I can't push it against the wall. My only other option is to push two chairs against the side of the bed with their backs pressing up against it. I'll be on the other side, and Katherine will be between. In a pinch, it seems like it will work.

It's a little earlier than her usual bedtime, and we don't have the luxury of CNN or MTV that we had back at the Army Guesthouse. I realize that I haven't sung to her yet, and scan my memory. What do I feel like singing? No *Twinkle-Twinkle*, no *Mary Had a Little Lamb*. I'm not in a nursery rhyme mood tonight. For no particular reason, what pops first into my head is the Beatles. *Sergeant Pepper's Lonely Heart Club Band*, to be precise.

"It was twenty years ago today," I begin. My voice echoes flatly off the naked walls. I move on to "What would you do if I sang out of tune, would you stand up and walk out on me…."

I proceed to sing the entire *Sergeant Pepper's album*, sides A and B, floundering only a moment when I try to remember if *Being for the Benefit of Mr. Kite* comes before *She's Leaving Home and Fixing a Hole*, or if it's the other way around. Katherine is transfixed (she has excellent taste). She stares at my lips, and is trying to process what is coming out of them.

By the time I get done holding the discordant ending note, she is still awake. We're lying on our sides facing each other on the bed. She watches expectantly. I search my memory bank. "I'm as restless as a willow in a windstorm…," I begin with the first strains of *It Might as Well Be Spring*. I plan on passing on to her my love of Standards too. By the time I finish *Dream a Little Dream of Me*, a song that I always swore that I would sing to my children someday, she is out, her lashes lay softly on her cheeks and her lips slightly part to allow her breath to whisper through them.

I AM SUCKED FORCEFULLY awake from a deep, deep sleep and am instantly totally coherent and alert. Something must have awakened me, but I don't at first hear anything. All of my senses, however, are heightened and tingling. Katherine still sleeps beside me. I lie motionless, waiting, barely breathing. It is so dark that I can't make out any features of the room, can't even see Katherine's body. I just feel it, feel her warmth radiating across the few inches that separate us.

I hear a rustling over near the wall to the left of the bed. Katherine's side. Lying there, I don't feel afraid, I feel leonine. *If I have to protect this little girl...* I mentally try to recall if any of my bags are over there. No, that's where those two chairs were. There's nothing there... The rustling stops. Perhaps a rat. I've seen my share of rats these past couple of weeks, dead in gutters, alive near garbage piles, along the banks of the river.

Suddenly I hear "Eeeeeeeeeeeek! Eeeeeeeeeeeeeeeeek! Eeeeeeeeeeeeeeek!" Loud, shrill, eerie screeching, and the sound moves lightning fast past the foot of my bed and out through the doorway into the bathroom that I can't see, but that I know is there, then down the hall towards the kitchen, squealing, squealing out the front of the house and fading away. I can follow the path the squealing makes because the rooms link circuitously, and the squeals echo off the walls and through the house.

Bigger than a rat. That *couldn't* have been a rat. Fast it traveled, without stopping. And I didn't hear it hit anything, didn't hear any doors move. It didn't sound like anything that I have ever heard before, not a cat, not a dog...

Katherine sleeps. I push the button on my Indiglo watch and it reads 2:34 a.m. I know that it was only moments between my waking, the rustle and the frenzied shrieking escape from the house, but time took on the expansion that heightened awareness can create. I continue to lie utterly still, feeling Katherine's undisturbed presence. Other than her barely audible exhale, there is solid, enveloping silence. The tingling alertness is gone, and I feel my muscles slowly relax.

Funny, I could have sworn that I had closed the door to the bathroom, and I *know* that the door between the bathroom and the hallway is shut. Otherwise, we would be open to the whole house. But oddly enough, I don't have much trouble falling back asleep. I don't feel afraid, and I don't have the urge to get up and investigate or to set up an all-night vigil.

When I wake up again, the normal way, it is getting light. I can see the features of the room. The door to the bathroom is, as I remembered, shut. Latched. No crack beneath the door, no hole in the wall. I get up and go to the bathroom to wash my face. The second door between the bathroom and the outer hallway is also closed. After drying my face, I go back into the room and begin packing. I'm not superstitious, and I'm not obsessed by the paranormal. But there is no doubt in my mind that we met the house ghost last night, and from what I heard, we surprised it as much as it surprised me. Not a scary "Boo!" ghost. Just one hanging around from what I am sure is a very interesting past that this house has. But I have no desire to meet it again.

When Trung shows up around 7:30, my bags are on the porch. "I'm sorry," I tell him. "I'll pay you for last night, but Katherine was too cold, and I think the place scares her a little. There's no crib. I'm going to have to find somewhere else." Not a peep out of me about ghosts…I wonder what he would say? Oh, that's just old Uncle Kim? He died twenty years ago but still hangs out here from time to time? All Vietnamese homes have an ancestral alter, a place where the living offer respect for those who have passed on, but whose spirits continue to watch over the family, or cause mischief if they are not pleased. Or would he think that this American woman was a little nuts, turn me into the authorities and say I was unfit to be adopting one of their nation's children?

"You're right," he says instead, "this place is not good for babies. I will help you find another place where she will be happier." His expression is very concerned. Above all, the baby must be happy and comfortable. "My sister will watch her. We will go to see a place not too far from here."

We hop on the motorbike, and in a few blocks pass a morning market alive with shoppers buying produce. The bike slips in the mud where the pavement temporarily discontinues, and I tighten the grip of my knees on the seat. We turn another corner, and in front of us is a hotel, about15 stories high. Much more what I have in mind. Trung goes in with me, and even negotiates a few dollars off of the room rate for me, from $27 to $23 a night. Like the Army Guesthouse back in Hue, they will do my laundry for me. And they have CNN.

KATHERINE AND I SETTLE into our new digs. There is a large window that takes up one whole wall, and we can see the market, a major intersection and a cyclo waiting area. The river is behind the hotel *just a short walk away*, the man at the front desk assures me. Holding Katherine on my hip, we point together at the activity going on below us. The cyclos are getting out their rain gear; the clouds are weeping again.

Later, in a plastic-covered cyclo, we head over to the Binh Minh hotel. This is where Allen will be staying, and I want to leave him a note telling him where we are. It is a decidedly backpacker-crowd kind of place, with rooms going for about $12 a night. As I write out a note for Allen, telling him the name and number of our hotel, the front desk clerk hands a note to me.

"Mr. Allen called and said to give this message to an American woman that would come looking for him." It is a note saying that he will be delayed one more day, and will be arriving tomorrow instead. I leave my note, and enclose a card from my hotel. They serve breakfast at the Binh Minh, in a room with French doors that open out to the street. I sit down for a lingering cup of café *sua* with bread as Katherine sits on my lap. I feed her little bits torn from the center of my baguette, and she licks butter off of the paper wrapper.

After a half hour, a Vietnamese man passing by on the sidewalk comes in and walks directly up to me. I've never seen him before. He has a very distinctive upturned nose.

"You are the lady who stayed at the guesthouse on Ly Thuong Kiet?" It's a statement more than a question. His voice is deep, and his English is good.

Startled, I respond slowly, "Yes…"

"My name is Tin. I am a friend of Trung's. He told me about you. I have a car for hire. If you need to hire a car for anything, I have a cell phone, call me. I give you a very good price." He searches his pockets for a piece of paper and writes a ten-digit number on it. How on earth did he find me? 'Look for the American lady wandering around with the Vietnamese baby,' I guess.

"Many of the tourist places hire out cars, but add on a percentage for themselves. I own my own car, so you pay less. We can go to the tombs, the DMZ, the beach, wherever you want." He is not nagging and pestering like so many are when they come up and try to sell you something. I like him.

"I'll keep that in mind." I tell him. "I'll be in town for two weeks, and want to do some of those things, but not until it stops raining. I am meeting a friend tomorrow, and we will see what our schedule is. He may be needing a car as well." I tell him about our school, and how it is run by nuns from one of the pagodas, but I don't have details about where it's located. Tin doesn't know about it either.

While we are conversing, Katherine has continued to eat half of my breakfast. She is obviously graduating to real food. Tin is curious, as is everyone, about her.

"Lang Son? People are very poor in Lang Son," he repeats what I have heard over and over. "And she was born in the year of the dragon. That is very good! Every year is a different animal, and each one means something special. I was born in the year of the pig. The dragon is very special, very powerful. It is good luck."

When he mentions that he was born under the sign of the pig, I can't help but to look at his face, at his upturned nose. Just a coincidence, but he is one of those people whose nostrils you can see when you're looking at them straight-on.

I definitely want to go to see the tombs. Rough Guide tells me that there are several tomb complexes of the old emperors located along the Perfume River in the countryside. The DMZ is the infamous Demilitarized Zone, the dividing line between North and South during the American War. It's a whole day trip though, and would probably not be terribly enjoyable for a small child. The beach? Tin tells me that it's less than an hour away. Perhaps the rain will let up. Perhaps. But this is Hue, the city with the highest rainfall annually in the country. And it *is* the rainy season.

Tin leaves, and Katherine and I grab another cyclo across the bridge to go to the Dong Ba Market. It is a huge two-story market that occupies several square blocks. You can get everything, *anything* here. Gold jewelry, antibiotics over the counter, produce, fish, flowers, custom-made shoes, clothing, American food products, fabric, diapers, formula and babywipes (the three things I'm here for), candy and straw hats. Hue is known for its 'poem hats,' *non la* that are woven with a poem written on paper inserted between the layers. It is visible only when you hold it up to the light. Behind the market you will find hardware, furniture and automotive parts. If it can be had, it can be had at Dong Ba.

There are "scouts" here, Vietnamese who speak decent English who keep an eye out for Caucasians. When they see one, they offer to help them find what they are looking for. Then they get a kickback from whosever stall you purchased from later. The crazy thing about these markets is that there are no price tags. You are always trying to figure out about what you should be paying for something, trying to remember what you paid for the same thing before somewhere else, then haggle away. Always, *always* haggle.

Before I am inside the entrance, a scout has found me, a girl maybe in her early twenties, who does help me find my baby items, then leads me upstairs to a shop selling silk clothing. Robes, scarves, shirts, pants, dresses, *ao dais*. It turns out that the booth is owned by my scout's brother. No surprise there. But the prices seem good, five dollars for this, eight, ten for that — and all vibrantly colored silk. I am gift shopping, and walk away with about a hundred dollars worth of stuff. My 'scout' helps me carry bags back down the stairs, and I carry Katherine. And more bags. She parts the sea of people for us, and we make our way out into the fresh air. The cyclo driver spots me and hurries over, passing bags to me underneath the plastic sheeting once Katherine and I are settled. I wonder if somehow he gets a kickback, too.

Chapter opening photograph: Window detail
Forbidden City, Hue, Vietnam

五

Chapter 6

THE NEXT AFTERNOON, we head to the Binh Minh to meet up with Allen. I push Katherine the five blocks in the stroller with a rain poncho draped over the front, and another one keeping me dry as well. He should have had time to check in and drop his stuff in his room by now. When we get there, he is sitting in the dining area, going through some papers.

"Hi Ellen...Helloooooo, Katie!" He is excited to see her. On her part, she's still not too sure about the facial-hair thing. He immediately starts in with a game of peek-a-boo and touch-your-nose-like-this. She gets drawn in and becomes more animated.

"I'm not going to call her Katie, Allen. It's *Katherine.*"

I'm ignored. They are giggling. I let them play for a little while and order a café *sua*, slowly stirring the pale white syrup into the coffee. I'm craving the caffeine today. After a little over a week of disturbed sleep (with or without ghosts), I'm starting to feel worn down, perhaps coming down with a cold. And Katherine still fights bedtime for a half hour each night, and requires me to either be on the go or entertaining her in some way at all other times. My showers, reading and sleep all revolve around her conscious and unconscious moments. She's wonderful and her disposition is happy 97% of the time, but she is incapable of entertaining herself even for a moment. That's my job.

Allen and I head to the Internet Café around the corner, picking up some pastries at a shop on the way. In many countries, including Vietnam, people can't afford to own computers, let alone the access service. So there are Internet cafes where people can access their Yahoo! or Hotmail accounts, drink a coffee or soda, and pay for the service by the minute. The shop has a great price, 150 *dong* per minute — pennies. Many of the hotels charge up to 2,000 *dong*!

As Allen signs on to the computer, I sit next to him with Katherine on my lap. She is looking over my shoulder, and starts flirting with the teenage boy who is working there. Cluck, cluck, he goes. She ducks behind me and looks back. Peek-a-boo, she is playing, and he covers his own eyes with his hands. My head is her visual barrier. She giggles, smiles, coos and ahhhs, and her face scrunches up. She *knows* how irresistible she is. The girl working with him joins in, and soon they come over to meet her.

"What a lovely baby!" the girl exclaims.

"This is Katherine Huong," I tell them. My pronunciation has finally shaped up.

"Huong! Katherine *Huong*! Like the river!" they say, and the girl reaches for her. To my surprise, Katherine reaches her arms out in return. I pass her over, relieved to have a few moments' break.

They whisk her back to the desk, and proceed to amuse her with the papers there, a plant nearby, paintings for sale on the wall, and, of course, peek-a-boo. I feel light. No one is in my arms or on my lap or anywhere near my physical body. No one demanding anything of me, and I feel scandalous, enjoying a stolen bit of time.

I watch Allen typing away, and decide to sign on myself to check my own e-mail. I read through lots of well-wishes from everyone who read about Lily-then-Katherine and I being together. There are lots of demands for pictures, and I make a mental note to take a couple of finished rolls to the developers. There are several such places on this block.

I spend a half-hour on the computer, glancing up from time to time to watch the teenagers playing with Katherine. This place also has tables set out by the sidewalk, and there the regulars can sit with their café, lemon water, tea or soda. Katherine has become the source of conversation and amusement among them. With my computer time at 150 *dong* per minute, and free babysitting service, I think that I will be a regular here.

HEADING BACK TO THE BINH MINH (which means Sunrise), we dodge raindrops. Allen and I try to locate another hotel for me. Again. In the course of 24 hours I have discovered that the place where I'm staying has hot water only sporadically, which became a big problem this morning after Katherine had a particularly messy diaper experience. Up until today, she has been enjoying her baths in the hotel sinks, but this morning she *had* to have a bath (if you know what I mean), and the water was icy cold. She screamed and cried and squirmed, and I tried to get it done as quickly as possible, but I don't want to have to put her through that again. Or worry about myself getting hot water in the few unpredictable spare minutes when I get to shower.

After visiting a few places, I choose the Thuan Hoa, a state-run hotel a block away from the Binh Minh. It is nice, clean, the hot water works, is ghost-free (as far as I can tell), and I have negotiated a $17 a night rate. I think that I'm getting the hang of this negotiating. It does get tiresome though, because for everything, everyday, you have to be on your toes. At least restaurant menus have written, fixed prices. We then meet up with Allen at the Mandarin Cafe. We share a fruit salad, rice, tofu with stir-fried veggies and French fries. This is his favorite spot from previous trips here. Tomorrow we will go to the school that I have heard so much about, and meet the Buddhist nuns who run it.

THE NEXT MORNING, Katherine and I head over to the Binh Minh, and I order café, bread and an omelet. Yesterday at the Mandarin, as she watched me eating my food, Katherine jabbed towards it with her index finger. She wanted what I had. So I placed a few pieces of tofu, with rice and a few french fries on a napkin on the tray of her stroller. I needed to give her seconds.

Now she points. She jabs that right index finger towards my bread. "Mmmmmmmmm! Mmmmmmmmmm!" her majesty demands. Then my eggs with cheese. Jab, jab. "Mmmmmmmmm! Mmmmmmmmm!" Her feet are desperately flaying, trying to find something to push against, to lift her higher out of the stroller seat. "Mmmmmmmmmmmmmmmmmmmm!" Straight from the bottle to people food. That's fine with me. No worries about paying for and toting around little glass bottles of puree du jour, what we at home call babyfood. I didn't even see any at Dong Ba, and would have had no idea how to haggle for it.

I FIND THE PHONE NUMBER that I have written on the back of my money conversion cheat sheet, and we call Tin. He is able to pick us up and take us to Long Tho Pagoda and arrives in a brown 80's model Toyota. The ride to Long Tho pagoda takes almost half an hour. Technically, it's still in Hue, but the outskirts of the city is divided into hamlets. The further we get from the main part of the city, the more bikes and foot traffic we see. The buildings now are only one story and are in little bursts and clusters, separated by rice paddies along the sides of the road. Tin drops us off at an archway. A concrete, upward-sloped pathway is beyond, leading to yet another set of arches. Allen says that in the old days, the temples and pagodas were given the high ground for protection. The high ground was the most valuable property, because the river floods and overflows its banks each rainy season. The temples would be safe.

We walk up the path, through a second set of arches, and towards two one-story structures. There are potted plants and trees throughout the courtyard. In the center is a large concrete basin that holds a fountain. Goldfish swim in the depths, and there is an 'island' in the center, covered with stones, moss, and tiny statues and pagodas. It is a tranquil not-so-still life, as water tumbles down from a miniature mountain brook.

Some tables with benches sit under the covered porches, but no one is to be seen. The courtyard is partially tiled, part concrete, and radiates coolness. There is no glass in the windows, no doors in the entrances — it is all open air. I faintly see a brown-robed figure move quietly inside the darkness of one of the far doorways. Allen heads for that one, and I follow pushing Katherine in the stroller with the back dropped down into a reclined position. She fell asleep in the car on the ride over.

Meeting a bunch of robed women with shaved heads is nothing new to me after spending two summer retreats in Plum Village. I love being around nuns. Their manners and habits are so relaxing, and being around them helps me to remember to be calm, relaxed and mindful. They smile much, but say little. They walk, move and perform the simplest tasks with deliberate, patient grace. Their lack of hair accentuates the expression in their eyes, and somehow seems to soften their faces.

Allen introduces me to the nuns as we share hot tea. Word has spread about their little surprise visitor and there are plenty of curious glances towards the stroller, but Sister Minh Thanh, the abbess, forbids anyone to go near it for fear of waking Katherine. Allen and the abbess go over some financial details that they have been e-mailing each other about with Christine, a Vietnamese-American translator, then decide to head straight over to the school to see how some new building project is coming along.

The walk over to the school is muddy due to the…rain. I leave Katherine asleep at the Pagoda under the watchful eyes of one of the novice nuns. Her face glowed with excitement when she was given this duty. I'm sure that it beats peeling vegetables in the kitchen or doing laundry. It is not everyday that such a little one comes for a visit!

There is a light but steady drizzle falling. The school is only 100 steps or so away; there are no 'blocks' here, so I don't know how else to measure it. We pass through the gated entrance and walk into a tiled courtyard. There is singing coming through an open doorway of one of the classrooms of the 'U' shaped building.

This is the school that our group has built, *L'Ecole de L'Aimee*, The School of the Beloved. There are 35 students, some with profound disabilities like cerebral palsey, some are deaf and mute, others with varying degrees of mental retardation. Some believe that this is a legacy from the American War. This area was dosed highly and repeatedly with Agent Orange and other chemicals and herbicides in an attempt to keep the border clear. However, Allen says that population-wise there is little difference from other areas of the world. Regardless, children with disabilities here receive little to no care, let alone education, due to lack of resources and the fact that there has been nowhere for anyone to learn how to work with them.

We peek into one of the doorways to watch the children work. They sit at desks, bent over white pages that they are trying to fill with writing and pictures, or raising their hands to answer the questions of a teacher. In the final room are the singing children whose voices we heard when we first passed through the gate. All of these children that we have seen were not able to attend any school prior to *L'Ecole de L'Aimee*. Many were not even able to feed or go to the bathroom by themselves when they arrived. Their parents work in the fields from dawn until dusk and they just do not have the time that these children require. Our goal is to try to teach the ones who are capable enough skills to be able to participate in society and support themselves in some way when they are adults.

Most of the children are from desperately poor families, their clothing threadbare with age. Some arrive each day without shoes. The nuns and teachers tell me that many of them are lucky to have food on the table each day, or that they get their only meal of the day here at the school.

I take some pictures and video of the school and children to show our group back home. Then the children have a recess, and they come flowing out of the rooms, happy, squealing and excited that there are new people to investigate. We take a group photo on the patio. One of the deaf mute girls, Kim, shows me how she can write her name and her sister's on a hand-held chalkboard. Then she shows me a little dance, which I videotape, where she kisses her hands, hugs her arms close, then waves. A teacher tells me it is a dance to a romantic song where the girl loses her love.

The boys especially come close, and try to touch and hang on to my clothing. They want to be near the nice American lady. They are also stalling for time, because they don't want their recess to end. It does though, and they are herded back into the classrooms by their teachers. Allen and I go into the meeting room with Sister Minh Thanh and start to unpack the boxes of supplies that Tin has unloaded from the trunk.

LATER IN THE AFTERNOON, parents begin arriving to pick up their children. Kim has come out on the porch and wraps her arms around my waist. I am holding Katherine; one of the nuns brought her over when she woke up from her nap. Kim points to Katherine, then to me, then to Allen. She has a questioning, quizzical look on her face. No, I shake my head, pointing back and forth between myself and Allen. No, we're not together. Not in the way she is thinking at least. Then she points to me and Katherine, and I nod yes, we are together. Then she points to me and opens her hands in front of herself, shrugging her shoulders. Who am I with? I point to myself and shake my head. I am with nobody. Once again she gives me the quizzical look and opens her hands palms up in front of her. Why? I respond by repeating the gesture back to her. I don't know either…

Her mother rides up into the courtyard on a bicycle. Before Kim gets on, I motion her mother to come over. I replay Kim's dance for her on the camcorder viewscreen. What I paid for this camera would feed their entire family for two years, I think to myself. I am positive that she has never seen such a thing, but she watches as Kim kisses and hugs and waves. When it finishes, I turn off the camera. She turns to me and bows. There are tears in her eyes. I hadn't expected something I consider so simple to touch her so. Now there are tears in mine. I bow back.

Back in town, I push Katherine down to the corner to pick up the developed film. When I return to the Binh Minh, Allen is sitting in the dining room with a couple he has just met there. Wolfgang and Heidi are Swiss, and traveling on a two-week holiday. It turns out that they belong to a Buddhist meditation group back home, also. As I flip through my photos, attempting to pick out the best two to have scanned and sent over the invisible Internet to everyone back home, he tells them about our group's projects. He also tells them that they may be able to share in evening meditation at 7:30 tonight at Tu Hieu pagoda, *Thay's* root temple. They are very interested and write down the name of the pagoda.

I leave Allen to go to the Internet café to send off my pictures and an e-mail. My new friends there whisk Katherine out of the stroller as soon as we roll up. They have crackers waiting for her at the desk. They scan the photos for me, and I get the chance to compose my first e-mail since leaving Hanoi.

> Subj: Raining, raining in Hue!
> Date: 12/26/01 9:59:42 AM
> From: Efitz
> To: Vietnam Group
> File:MommyandKatherine.jpg (190869 bytes)
> DL Time (32000 bps): < 2 minutes

Sent from the Internet (Details)

Hello All!

Finally! Pictures for everyone to see!!!

I have been in the city of Hue for the past three days. I love the slower pace! Katherine continues to enchant everyone she passes, and I have made many, many new friends because of her! :)

This is where the school is that our group in Norfolk built for disabled children...cerebral palsey, deaf, various degrees of mental retardation. It has been amazing to see them all, and I've been taking videos with my new digital camcorder to show people at home what they are giving money for. I taped one little deaf mute girl doing a dance, then played it back on the camera to show her mother...her mother cried. The children loved to see themselves played back on the video!

The level of poverty is staggering. Allen bought $100 worth of educational toys, blocks and puzzles in Hanoi, and it is riches for them. Most of the children have very thin, dirty clothes that they wear day after day. I'm thinking of doing a little shopping with one of the Vietnamese people (to negotiate good prices!), to buy clothes and supplies for the children. As I write all this, I think I will copy it and send it off to all my friends...maybe you guys would like to help out with $10, $20 (even that would be a HUGE difference!), then when I get back, you can pay me back. What do you think everybody???!!! Please let me know in the next few days..

A late Merry Christmas to everybody!

Love, Ellen

I HIT THE 'SEND' BUTTON, and have started a cause, as I am in the habit of doing. Perhaps I can spend a hundred dollars or so to help out some of the most needy children at the school. I'll use some of my money regardless, but if I can rustle up some dough out of my friends, that would be even better.

It's getting close to seven o'clock, and Allen's comment about joining the monks at Tu Hieu pagoda for meditation has been tempting me as I've been typing. I ask to use the phone to call Tin. If we can find Trung's sister to watch Katherine again, could he take me to the pagoda? He says he can, and will pick me up at the Internet café.

Now you might think Asian religion, and picture people sitting around on mats for days on end, without moving a muscle, meditating their way to enlightenment. I'm not the most dedicated meditator, but I do keep trying. Goes hand in hand with the think-too-much syndrome that I seem to be afflicted by. But *Thay's* approach is to *practice* the precepts of Buddhism throughout all of your daily activities, from work to play, from having a conversation with a friend to helping others — to being a parent. This approach has brought me to a more peaceful, relaxed place, and I don't have to feel bad about being a crummy meditator. I didn't say that I was a good Buddhist, but I'm a trying-to-be good Buddhist. One of the cool things about Buddhism is that it's OK to be a trying-to-be good Buddhist! That's why it's called Buddhist *practice*. Being able to sit tonight though, to breathe in peace and quiet and just sit, is just what I need after the frenzied past week and a half.

WHEN WE GET TO TRUNG'S, his sister is behind the house and agrees to watch Katherine. A couple dollars for her, which is about two days' wages! Trung, however, is nowhere to be found, and Tin is not sure which pagoda I am talking about. I tell him that I think I can remember the way. Down through a few lights, a left turn, over the railroad tracks. I see the familiar wide sidewalk.

Tin's Toyota can't get any closer than the edge of the street, and

I climb out of the door. Stepping out into the mud, I tell him to meet me back on this spot in two hours, at 9:15. It is drizzling, and I have on a hooded rain poncho. I walk the rest of the way down the unlit path. No one is around, and through the windows of the homes to my right I can see the blue glow of television sets and hear the clinking of plates and bowls, chopsticks and cups, as families finish their dinners. To my left are the railroad tracks with grasses and shrubbery thickly springing up along the edges.

When I reach the entrance to the pagoda below the arches, it is even darker. There is no light source nearby and I stand a moment to let my eyes adjust. Beyond the arches is the garden. I can't see it, but I know that it's there. There is no one around, no movement of any kind.

Standing there, feeling the rain hit the skin of my poncho, I try to tune in to see if I feel any apprehension, if there's any uneasiness about this dark place where I've only been once before. If I had never been here, I doubt that I would attempt the climb up the slope. But right now I feel no sense of danger, no scariness. In fact, I have not felt even the slightest fear *anywhere* since coming to Vietnam, even with the ghost. There is more of a peaceful closeness enveloping me, and I decide to start up the slippery moss-covered stones.

I begin along the edge, feeling my way along the stone wall, my right hand gripping into the damp, crumbly surface for balance. Even with this support my sneakers lose their traction a few times. I pass through the archway at the top and enter the garden. The trees and foliage are a little more visible now from the brightness of a mist that floats just above the ground. The soil is loose stones and dirt, and I decide that this is an appropriate time to practice mindful walking. In *Thay's* tradition, we practice mindful walking, or walking meditation, in which we slowly place one foot in front of the other, feeling the earth beneath our feet, not thinking about anything else other than our breathing, our steps, the earth below us and our relation to it. In my mind, I always envision walking on lily pads floating on a lake, where each time I step down, the pad can just barely hold my weight if I balance just so, and a few drops of water slosh over the edge of the leaf looking like little mercury droplets on the greenness.

Slowly I progress, barely making any sound with my lily-pad steps, toward the buildings that I know are along the back of the garden. Soon I am even with the covered kiosks, and I continue onward to where the outer temple is. There are no lights on anywhere, no sign of anyone. I realize abruptly that Trung had not brought me to the correct place two days ago, and that this is not Tu Hieu pagoda. I stop, pause long enough to decide not to continue on, then make my way back to one of the kiosks. At least I can stand out of the rain for a little while.

When I reach the nearest kiosk, I see that in the covered area in front there is a step before the opening in the building where the Buddha statue is. I sit on the step, thinking that it will be almost two hours before Tin comes, and I have no other way of reaching anyone. It is quiet here though, and peaceful, and from the direction of the main meditation hall I hear a gong, signaling the beginning of meditation session for the monks who are inside. I decide to sit meditation with these monks. Out here physically, but join them in spirit as they meditate in the temple that I cannot see off at the end of the garden.

Katherine is being watched, and I get a chance to breathe and not think about anything and not take care of anyone. I pull my legs into the cross-legged half-lotus position, being careful so the water that is on my poncho doesn't find its way into a crease and onto my dry clothes. I fold my hands palms-up in my lap, one cupped inside the other. I close my eyes as I draw in a deep, slow breath, feeling the air find its way all the way into the deepest, lowest recesses of my lungs. Though my eyes are closed, I feel and hear the garden. Feel the thickness of the moisture-laden misty air. Hear the raindrops as they trickle and descend down the leaves, the grasses, the trunks of the trees. The stone is cold beneath my body, but the air is just warm enough so that I don't feel chilled.

Long, slow, deep breath in. I feel as if I float with the air that I have taken into my body. Instead of the air becoming a part of me, inside of me, it's as if I've been lifted up to become a part of it, losing myself in it. I breathe out. I sit. I listen to the rain. I sit. In the distance, I can faintly hear the sound of the engines of the *sampan* boats on the river. Chop, chop, chop, chop. A thought briefly enters my mind that they sound like helicopters. Over thirty years ago, the skies of Hue rang with the sounds of helicopters and other war machines. What I hear tonight seems like a distant echo.

I gently push these thoughts away from my consciousness. I sit. I breathe. I hear crunching on the stones and dirt. My eyelids lift slowly. I see a figure coming towards me, from the direction of the temple. It is a brown-robed monk, and he follows the path that passes right in front of the kiosk. He doesn't see me. I am still and in the shadows. He continues on and disappears into the mist. I sit. I breathe. I am awash in gratitude to be able to be in this place right now. A place that was a mistake, yet is the most perfect thing.

Almost half a year ago on July 3rd, my 38th birthday, I sat down and pondered what I was going to do about wanting to be a mommy. I didn't have an other half, a partner in life that usually makes that possible. So I decided to make things happen on my own. I am now a mother. I am experiencing this beautiful country; I am in this place now, because I came to find my daughter, to find Katherine. Without even trying to, this little girl has given me a great gift. The first of many, I have no doubt. Of all the things that I have done in my life, this has altered it the most. Do I have plans? Sometimes I think so, sometimes I want to just go with the flow. Can I foresee the future? Not really. I just want to see what opens up before us.

More crunching. The monk returns. When he is once again even with the kiosk, something makes him lift his head, though I haven't so much as twitched. He stops. He sees me. All he can see is a seated, rain-ponchoed figure, face obscure in the dark. I raise my hands and place my palms together in front of me, in front of my heart, and bow. He bows, turns and continues on to the temple.

I sit. I breathe. All I am is here and now. My body sitting under this kiosk. Breathing. The past doesn't matter right now; the future doesn't matter right now. This moment is a still, full moment, and the more I pay attention to it, the more it expands to envelop me. It's not just peacefulness, it's…nothing…and everything. It just is. I breathe. I sit.

Chapter opening photograph: Sister Minh Thanh and Katherine

六

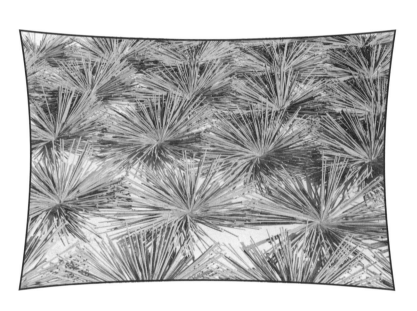

Chapter 7

WE CROSS THE PERFUME RIVER on the Trang Tien Bridge. I am on the back of a motorbike with my arms wrapped around the waist of a nun. The sleeves of her robe flap in the breeze, and her *non la* is secured firmly beneath her chin. So far she is beating our companions in the ride to the Dong Ba market where we are headed to do some serious shopping.

The response of my friends and family to my arm-twisting has netted us $350 to spend on the children of *L'Ecole de L'Aimee*. Traveling with me today are the Buddhist nun, a teacher from the school named Phuong, and Christine, the translator. Katherine is back at the Binh Minh under Allen's watchful eye. I hold the cash. My companions hold the shopping list, as they know the children well, and know who needs what.

Sister and I arrive at the market three lengths ahead of the other bike. The score is: me and the nun, 1; other guys, zip. To park the motorbikes they have to shell out 2,000 *dong* apiece, and the attendant writes their claim number on the black vinyl seat with white chalk. Sister immediately grabs my hand and the teacher hooks her elbow through my other arm. They maneuver me into the cavernous opening, and we are absorbed into the dimly lit interior, weaving around shoppers, scouts and stalls. The scouts glance at me, but they have no chance of capturing me now!

First we head to one of the jewelry stalls to change American money into *dong*. They give the best rates my companions tell me, especially if you have a couple of crisp new U.S. hundreds. In Vietnam, I have noticed, the U.S. dollar is the second currency of the nation. Every shop, vendor and taxi driver are more than willing to take U.S. money at 15,000 *dong* to the dollar.

Once our money is changed, we head upstairs to where the clothing stalls are. It is cramped and crowded upstairs. The stalls are arranged row after row, with each stall space being perhaps ten feet wide. The rows themselves are less than three feet wide, so when people pass each other, it is often a body-rubbing close encounter. In every direction there are people standing at the stalls on each side of the aisle, and people trying to squeeze between them attempting to pass. Nobody seems to have a particularly strong sense of personal space here.

We wander up and down a few aisles, scoping out who has what, and checking what we see against what we need on the scrawled list. Sister, the teacher and Christine have matched children's names to jackets, dresses, pajamas — whatever they think that child needs most. If there's money left over, we'll get some bookbags, too.

They settle on a stall along the back wall. The woman who runs it, Sister and Phuong get down to some serious bargaining. Christine and I stand back to watch the exchange. Although we fight it, we keep getting pressed up into the next stall by the passing crowd that constantly flows through the aisle like a tidal surge. Items are taken off hooks, examined and replaced. Bags of clothing appear and disappear again from under the recesses beneath the table. The woman at the next stall, who's not getting our business and is less than pleased that we are blocking the view of her merchandise, keeps waving us off. She has a long stick with a hook on the end that she uses to reach the very high items hanging from the sides of the stall. From time to time, she uses it to poke Christine and I in the shoulder and upper arm, trying to shoo us away, but we can't fight the press of bodies.

We finally decide to roam around on our own and check out fabric stalls and the candy sellers. I pick up a few bags of sweets for the teens at the Internet store. Ginger-sesame and banana chews, and candied sweet potato. When I tried to pay them some extra money the other day for helping with Katherine, they refused, saying "But we love the baby!"

We look through bolts and bolts of silk, bright, shiny, satiny silk. Soft, drape-y, ethereal silk. Red with dragons! Black with gold bamboo. I would love to get a few more outfits made. Christine succeeds in holding me back from purchasing anything.

"Let's wait until the Sister and Phuong are free. We don't want to get ripped off."

Back at negotiations, they are racking up an impressive pile of loot. The stall-keeper is stuffing folded clothing into garbage bags. One million eight hundred thousand *dong*, a hundred and twenty dollars, has bought three garbage bags full of clothing. I count out eighteen one hundred-thousand *dong* notes. The owner asks my friends something in Vietnamese, and they respond. She smiles at me as we walk away, inclining her head in a little bow. They tell me she wanted to know who I was, and that she liked my tall nose. *An American friend, here to buy clothes for the children at the school*. And, thanks to my Hungarian ancestry, a tall nose is absolutely what I have.

We move on to another stall, this one at the end of a row near the center stairway. There's a little more breathing room here, even little red plastic stools to sit on. I pull one up beside the table, trying to stay out of the traffic pattern. It's so low that my elbows rest comfortably on my knees. Out of the corner of my eye I catch something black as it darts out from under another table, through the legs of my stool, then disappears. A rat. It moves so fast that I don't even have a chance to flinch as it scurries inches from my feet.

BACK OUT IN FRONT OF THE MARKET, we reclaim the motorbikes and stand looking back and forth between the bikes, the three loaded garbage bags, and the four of us. With a few attempts, we finally settle on one bag between the Sister's feet, me behind her, and one on the other bike between Phuong's feet. The last is wedged between her and Christine who is riding behind her. Not an eye is batted by anyone passing by as we bounce down the curb. Precarious cargo carriage on two-wheeled vehicles is standard operating procedure in Vietnam. For the same thing in the U.S., I have no doubt that we would be pulled over and ticketed. But we're not in the U.S. And we're not ready to go home yet.

When Christine tells them about the silk that we looked at, and that I would like to have some clothing made, they tell me about a tailor shop not far away. There I can pick out some designs and they will tell us how much fabric I will need to buy. We head upriver what turns out to be six blocks away, to Phuong Mai, a tailor shop run by two sisters. They are around the corner from a restaurant owned by their brothers on Dinh Tien Hoang. The restaurant is packed. It is hard to find a spot on the sidewalk for the motorbikes, but we manage to squeeze them in, rolling over some plywood placed over a torn-up spot in the sidewalk. Entering the shop, our Sister greets the two tailor sisters. Christine finds out that before our school was built, the nuns held an informal school that the two attended. Both sisters are hearing impaired — completely deaf, as are the brothers who own the restaurant. At that time, children who were not able to keep up with non-disabled students did not have the opportunity to learn anywhere else. Even now, most of the programs for these children are run by groups like ours or other charitable organizations, although that is slowly changing.

The sisters measure me, then ask me to flip through several pattern books. I choose to have two long gowns made, each of which will require two meters of fabric. There is no need for translation today. Without having to rely on Vietnamese spoken language, everything is done by pointing, writing numbers and hand motions. I have an easier time here communicating with these women than in most other places I have been. After a conference, we decide to go back now and buy the fabric, since I already know the stall where I want to buy it.

People and bags go back on the bikes. Six blocks and we're back in front of Dong Ba. Phuong stays in front with the motorbikes and bags of clothes, and once again Sister takes me by the hand. Back up the stairs. We go to the stall that is piled to over six feet high with bolt after bolt of cloth. I run my hands over this pattern and that, the shopkeeper pulls out one, then another, and Christine, Sister and I unfold and drape and examine. We choose my first picks from earlier, the red with dragons and the black with gold bamboo. Sister does all the talking. They settle on a price. 22,000 *dong* per meter…less than two dollars! Sister tells Christine, Christine translates to me, and I pull the money out of my fannypack. The stall-keeper looks a little pained as he hands me the plastic bag of folded fabric. He adds something in Vietnamese, and we smile and leave. When we get downstairs, Christine tells me that he said that he normally gets much more from a foreign lady. She said that I paid nun's price because he said that he couldn't lie to the Sister. I also have no doubt that Sister, with her young face never breaking from its serene bearing, is a ruthless negotiator. I file that away for future useful information: if you need to shop, take a Sister with you. No one can stand up to haggling with a nun.

Fortunately, the ride back to the Binh Minh is only over the bridge, then three blocks further down Hung Vuong. Allen, as I expected, has spent the past two hours at the Internet café. Katherine is giggling with our friends, and is happy to share a piece of soft banana candy when I give them the bag from the market. Allen tells me that he plans to go to Tu Hieu pagoda, the *real* Tu Hieu, tonight to sit meditation with the monks. I had told him about my experience the other night, adding that it ended up being just what I needed after all. But I still want to go experience the real thing. We call Tin's cell phone and ask him to pick us up at six o'clock.

Tu HIEU IS ALMOST HALF AN HOUR OUTSIDE of town, and is surrounded by a pine forest. This most definitely is not the place that Trung took me.

"Oh, *this* is where you wanted to go the other night!" Tin says. "Why didn't you tell me *Tu Hieu*? It's in all the guidebooks. We always take tourists up here."

Because I didn't remember the name! Like I'm supposed to possess a short-term memory while experiencing sleep deprivation and the newness of mommyhood.

Tin drops us at a triple-arched gate with a tranquil pond behind it. Lilies are scattered on the smooth dark surface like tossed breadcrumbs. Late afternoon sunlight filters and dapples through the high pine branches. It is a short walk up to the pagoda through the woods. The first steps rise right out of the leaves and pine needles of the forest floor. Two steps to get up over a little wall. A stone terrace. A few more steps. Another terrace. There are several buildings, the one furthest to the left is the temple. It has a wide opening on the front that is covered by wooden doors in the evening and during bad weather, but right now they are pushed back to the sides. We go instead to the building on the right, which serves as a study hall for the monks and a meeting place. Not all of the monks speak English, but Allen has a piece of paper with a name written down on it of one who does: Tu Niem. He shows the paper to a young novice who rises from reading a book. He departs and returns shortly with another young monk. The new monk has a broad calm smile and dark bushy eyebrows…and a shaved head of course.

All of the ordained monks and nuns have shaved heads. I have seen the nuns wearing either gray or brown robes. The monks I see are only wearing brown. The young novice nun that helps to watch Katherine at Long Tho pagoda has a shaved head except for a long handful of bangs. These are long enough for her to loop over her ear. She will be allowed to shave this when she is fully ordained.

Tu Niem greets us and says that the Abbot will be joining us shortly, but in the meantime we visit in the study hall at one of the long tables with benches. He brings a tray of candied ginger, and makes a pot of tea from hot water in a thermos. Lotus tea, he says. While we wait for the abbot and for the tea to brew, we chat about what we have been doing on our trip. I tell him the story of how I have come to Vietnam to adopt a little girl, and where Katherine came from. He is intrigued. "What a very special thing to do," he tells me.

Tu Niem rises as he sees the Abbot, Thich Chi Mau, approach. We do the same. The Abbot has a broader smile than Tu Niem, and a broader belly as well. He speaks no English and relies on Tu Niem to translate for us. Mostly he chooses not to talk, but just sits there and is content to smile and be in our presence. After an exchange between them, Tu Niem turns back to me.

"Sister, the Abbot says that he is touched by the story of your baby. He says that he would like to meet her, if you come back to the pagoda again." Since I am a Buddhist layperson, a person who practices Buddhism but has not taken formal vows to be a nun or monk, Tu Niem calls me 'sister.' He has shared our story with the abbot.

Yes, I will bring her back here. I would like to come back to this place. It is very peaceful here. I turn to the Abbot and incline my head in a little bow. He does the same in return.

"We would like to sit meditation with the monks tonight, if that is possible," Allen says. Tu Niem nods his assent.

"Yes, that will be possible. Meditation is at seven thirty. It will be soon. I will take you back to the meditation hall."

The Abbot continues to sit and smile. He enjoys the candied ginger. We all sip our lotus tea in silent, unhurried company from the small cups for a few more moments.

When we rise, we bow to the Abbot. Tu Niem leads us through some of the open folded doors and out into a courtyard. Like at Long Tho, there are dozens of potted plants and trees of various sizes. There is also a pond, and a raised concrete basin with a gnarled vine-like tree growing up from the middle of it.

"Starfruit," Tu Niem says, pointing up to the pale yellow and golden fruit hanging in the branches overhead. "This vine is over one hundred years old." He reaches up and there is the soft snap of bark breaking as a fruit separates from its perch. He presents it to me, and I raise the smooth skinned fruit to my nose. It smells faintly of roses. I thank him. I will save it for later as a special mindful treat.

As we wind around the buildings, evening is coming fast and the forest canopy hastens the darkness. There is little light, and Tu Niem takes Allen's hand to help lead him. I have noticed that in Vietnam it is very common and comfortable for men to be physically demonstrative to other men. In Hanoi, I often saw teenagers and men standing or walking down the street with their arms draped over each others' shoulders. As a monk, it would also not have been appropriate for him to grab hold of my hand.

After turning yet another corner, we bump into a group of young novice monks, who I would guess to be around ten or eleven years old. They are giggly and a bit rambunctious, shoving each other, until they realize they aren't alone. They fall silent, snap straight to attention, and shuffle away with quick steps.

When we arrive at the meditation hall, Tu Niem pardons himself and leaves us, and we linger outside a few minutes. We add our shoes to the growing rows at either side of the door. Monks young and old are making their way into the hall. The older monks are wearing orange robes now, instead of their daily wear brown. The novices don't get orange robes yet. Tu Niem must have gone to change.

Barefoot, I step freely through the doorway of this place where my teacher, Thich Nhat Hanh, was trained and ordained as a monk over thirty years ago. He now lives in Plum Village in the Bordeaux region of France, a community of monks and nuns and lay-practitioners. That is where I first saw him and heard him speak a few years ago. It was during the summer retreat where visitors can come and live and practice for a while in this *sangha*, the community of Plum Village.

Before going to the retreat, I had read and enjoyed several of *Thay's* books. That first day I sat down cross-legged on the floor, about 15 feet off to *Thay's* right as he sat on the raised platform. There he was, in his brown robe, with a thermos of hot tea by his side, without the tiniest bit of hurry or concern for procedure. He smiled, glanced slowly around, adjusted his mike, took a long, slow breath, and looked around a little more. When he finally started to speak, he taught us how to breathe. He told us that even though we had been doing it our whole lives, we did not know how to do it right. That through gaining full awareness of our breathing, we can calm our body, our mind and our thoughts. We can learn to create harmony and ease in our lives. Awareness of our breath brings us to the present moment, and it is only in the present moment that we can experience peace and happiness.

All these years, and I hadn't been breathing right. That day I drew into my lungs one long, slow, pure, totally conscious, enlightened breath. I had never taken such a breath before, and have not experienced it again. It felt like my lungs could keep expanding forever, encompassing the whole universe. I still remember that breath like it was just a few moments ago instead of the almost four years that have since passed. And it's funny that such a seemingly small thing, that *one breath*, continues to be a touchstone in my life. "One doesn't become enlightened and stay that way," another Zen master, Suzuki Roshi, said. "If you are lucky, life is a series of little enlightenments." Through breathing, through being aware and present and paying attention to the life that I live right now, I can sometimes catch these moments of lucidity, these little enlightenments. And when it happens, that is true peace. But it is a daily practice, requiring constant reminders, to live up to the *Dharma* name, the spiritual name, that I received in Plum Village: Mindful Path of the Heart.

When Tu Niem returns, he is wearing orange, and he leads us inside, instructing us to sit in the back rows with the novices. It doesn't surprise me when I see that I am the only female here. Monks and nuns live and practice separately, and a visiting western female layperson is an infrequent occurrence. But nobody does anything to make me feel as if this is unusual. No one even gives me a second glance, even furtively—even the novices. I am just another person here to sit with them.

I find a cushion and take a seat on the aisle directly behind the last row of orange-robed backs. There is dim lighting and incense burning. The ceiling is vaulted, which makes the shuffling of the last arrivals echo softly. It is not cushy, nor is it austere. It is pleasantly open and vacant in the large room. A few photos of robed monks and spiritual teachers hang on the front wall, and, of course, a statue of the Buddha on the simple altar. But there is not so much stuff that your mind can stop and settle on anything for too long. A bell sounds, signaling the beginning of our sitting session.

I relax into the half-lotus position, legs crossed, left foot pulled up a little higher to rest on top of my right thigh. I take a deep, long breath in…and let it slowly release. Ahhhhhhhh, is the feeling in my mind, in my body. I am in this place where my teacher was trained decades ago. I am sitting surrounded by men who have dedicated their life to contemplation, study and practicing mindfulness. To learning and practicing and following the Dharma, the Buddhist path, the path to enlightenment.

When I am back home, I will try to remember to think of this place sometimes, of the monks practicing here. Part of their practice is to meditate, to live with mindfulness, to practice, not just for themselves, but for the whole world. Peace on an individual level, no matter who you are or where you are, contributes to peace everywhere. The presence of peace spreads its energy outward like ripples on the surface of water. They are here practicing for me too.

My breath comes effortlessly. I am filled with joy and peace to be in this place. I don't even feel my arms, my legs. The tension that sometimes comes from sitting this way, sitting still, unmoving, is not there. There is nothing.

Breathing in, I know that I am breathing in. Breathing out, I know that I am breathing out. There are no thoughts in my mind other than thinking about the air passing into my lungs, expanding them, my ribs separating to accommodate the expansion, how my chest rises, how my head and neck and back lift ever so slightly, then, pause, and then I relax my muscles, my chest, let my rib cage compress in, and how these processes naturally squeeze the air back out, not forcefully, but in a steady, relaxed stream. Feeling the sensation of all of this happening, only to pause and to begin all over again. Breathing in, breathing out. Breathing in, breathing out. This is all there is, right here, right now.

AT EIGHT O'CLOCK, an electric clock chimes. Not something romantic like a gong or a bell, but very artificial-sounding electric tones, from a very gaudy-looking electric clock, shiny gold plastic, that I hadn't noticed sitting unobtrusively up front on the floor to the right. Odd. What an odd way to break this silence.

All right. I confess. No, I did *not* sit in ecstatic bliss for the whole half hour. At some point, I just couldn't stand it and slowly lifted my eyelids. I wanted to *see* where I was, see the monks sitting in stone statue-stillness. To see the walls and the thin stream of smoke drifting towards the ceiling from the burning incense. I wanted to bring that back with me in my memory, not just a feeling I had when my eyes were closed.

It was comforting to see row after row after row of orange-robed backs and shaved heads. There was the tiniest bit of noise coming from the ranks of novices sitting behind me. Then, up ahead of me, in the third row almost all the way to the left, I saw a movement. I saw an orange-clad arm lift, and a hand reach up to scratch an eyebrow. Eureka! I am liberated! Me, the lousy meditator (well, these past few times have been pretty good) can get off my own back. For years I have been chastising myself. If I was a good enough meditator, I would not even *feel* an itch, let alone to have to reach up to scratch it. I wouldn't *hear* distracting noises. I should somehow be so enraptured in some alternate reality bliss that my purely mortal body would stop being mortal. But here, now, I see a purely mortal orange-robed body with a very mortal itch. What do you do when you're meditating and you have an itch? You scratch it, instead of sitting there thinking that you have an itch, that somehow you shouldn't have an itch and trying not to scratch it. Just scratch it. Then breathe.

ALLEN AND I LINGER, waiting in line to get our shoes, Tu Niem finds us once again. He shows me a piece of paper. "The story about your baby so touched me that I was unable to meditate," he says. "Instead, I wrote her a poem." I look at the paper. It is written in Vietnamese. "When you come back with your baby Katherine, I will have it translated for you. I will write it out better than this."

Thank you, I tell him, feeling very honored. With everything that I have been through to find Katherine, and what we have been through together since I came to Vietnam, it just feels to me like we are following where our path leads us. First what I needed to do, and now what we need to do together to get from day to day. Nothing special.

I get back to the hotel with Katherine later than usual that night, but she seems like she'll be happier with one more bottle before sleep. There is no hot pot at this hotel, but the maids have remembered each day to refill the thermos with hot water. I mix up a bottle, and settle in with Katherine on the bed in our customary position. The calm feeling from the meditation hall continues to linger in my mind. We play one of the little games that we have invented. As she drinks, she draws in one short, noisy inhalation, watching me intently, expectantly. Not quite a snort, I call it a huff. I pause and huff back at her. She smiles, still drinking, so not really a smile, it's more that her eyes crinkle up. She waits a few moments, adding to the suspense, then....huff! back at me. I smile back "yi! yi! yi! yi!" I say, and hug and squeeze her body in close to mine. She smiles again, then we both become serious. She waits. I wait, looking at her without blinking, then 'Huff!' I huff back at her, and her eyes crinkle up all over again. Huff! Huff! This can amuse us for a good half hour, this give-and-take communication game that we have happened upon. She always waits for her turn, no matter how long I pause. And she increases her pauses as well, timing her response, becoming very serious, then laughing all over again. She continues to amaze me.

THE NEXT MORNING, rain is tickling the windows, keeping me in a lulled half-sleep. The overcast skies make it seem earlier than it is by blocking out any sunrays that might be up there, somewhere, trying to find their way down to Hue. It is eight-fifteen. Katherine still slumbers, snoring a little on her belly, and I give her a jealous glance. I almost feel like giving her a poke, a little disturbance, in return for the three crying fits that she kept me awake with last night.

Now that wasn't a very motherly or mindful thought, I tell myself. But so many nights of disturbed sleep is starting to wear on my immune system. My throat is sending sharp messages up to my ears with every swallow that I take, and sniffles keep me stuffing my pockets with tissues. Getting sick is *not* an option. I turn over and enjoy a few more minutes of peace, listening to the slosh of mud under the wheels of vehicles, two-wheeled and four, passing by outside of my window.

After our usual breakfast with Allen at the Binh Minh, the three of us head to Long Tho pagoda. There really isn't anything for me to do at the school, but back in town I would have to entertain Katherine all day by myself.

Once at the pagoda, my yawns give me away, and I tell Christine that I'm not feeling very well. She passes this information on to Sister Minh Thanh, who immediately summons the novice with the looping bangs. Before I can say a word, I watch her retreating back as she pushes Katherine's stroller down one of the covered walkways. Christine takes my hand and leads me to her room.

"Lay down and rest here," she tells me, and I gratefully sink down onto the edge of her bed. "And don't worry about the baby!" She closes the folding accordion door behind her, leaving me in a simple, tiny room that can barely hold a bed, some shelves and a trunk.

Once on my back, I notice that the walls don't go all the way up to the peaked roof, leaving a triangular gap open to the outside. There are also a couple of inches of space under the bottom of the door. I can hear the daily life of the pagoda as my head rests on the pillow. Muffled voices from a few rooms away as Allen, Christine and Sister Minh Thanh discuss the building project at the school. The clinking of dishes, pots and pans as breakfast is cleaned up and lunch is prepared. The continued tap, tap, tap of the raindrops on the roof that has almost been dismissed by my ears as irrelevant background noise. The slap of plastic sandals on wet concrete as someone passes by. Someone else is in the bathroom brushing their teeth. Far away, I think I catch a giggle from Katherine.

Not much privacy here, I think, but somehow I feel comforted and cradled to hear life going on around me, like individual cells all doing their part to keep the larger organism healthy and functioning. I feel a part of the organism as well, a sense of connectedness, of belonging. Perhaps that is part of the problem back home in the States, in the land of Prozac and Paxil. Too much privacy. Too much separateness. Too much aloneness. Too many people not truly belonging or being connected to anyone or anything.

I lay still in the timeless twilight between sleep and wakefulness, enveloped in this engulfing reverie of sounds. Time and thoughts and sounds and feeling blur together. When I finally rise and step towards the folding door, I glance at my watch to discover that three hours have passed. I feel wonderfully relaxed and refreshed.

On the covered patio, I find Allen, Christine and a few of the nuns at a table having lunch. "We didn't want to wake you," Christine says, to which I can only manage a delirious smile in return. I sit down and join the feast. On the table are stacks of several kinds of spring rolls, both soft and fried, noodle dishes, rice, tofu chunks and strips in sauce, vegetables, cooked greens, dumplings and soup. No meat to be found, which is just fine with me. We talk, we eat, we laugh, the rain falls from the sky. I breathe. I smile.

Subj: Vietnam Donations
Date:12/30/01 6:03:47 PM
From: Efitz
To: Vietnam Group
Sent from the Internet (Details)

Greetings!

Just wanted to give everyone an update on the donations. We've spent a few days shopping, and have bought clothes, jackets, book bags, etc. for 35 children, and still have some money to spare for school supplies. It was SO MUCH fun in an unbelievably crowded market, with people pushing by, three of us and a Buddhist Nun (having a nun with you gets the best price! ;)). We carried out garbage bags full of clothes. Many of these kids have never owned anything brand new.

Love, Ellen

BACK IN TOWN THAT EVENING, the rain seems to have finally let up. After leaving the Internet shop, I push Katherine's stroller towards the river. The sky darkens and the streets shimmer, reflecting the lights along Le Loi. I want to catch another glimpse of the candles that are sure to be sent floating down the surface of the river soon. On my right, I pass the entrance to the Saigon Marin, an upscale hotel near the foot of Trang Tien bridge. Twinkling lights in the lobby attract my attention, and I bump the stroller backwards up several stairs to the front door to investigate.

Inside I find a large artificial Christmas tree with wrapped boxes underneath in red and gold. The tree is covered with dozens of votive candles, and it glows and glitters in the dimly lit room. Katherine rests on my hip as we stand admiring the beauty if it. Around us, well-dressed tourists pass by.

Then, a group of formally dressed Vietnamese come to stand by the tree. A very rotund middle-aged man dressed in a crisply pressed gray suit stands to the other side of the tree to have his picture taken. He smiles broadly, which makes his full cheeks puff up even more. He has the self-assured air of a politician or government bureaucrat. After the flash goes off, he relaxes his pose, looks towards me, and we smile at each other. He comes over with a few words for Katherine.

"You adopt baby?" he struggles to say in halting English.

"Yes," I reply.

"Ah! Lucky baby!" he exclaims, and turns to his friends speaking in Vietnamese. The camera is raised again, and the click captures the three of us standing in front of the sparkling tree.

As the round man and his entourage make their way out of the lobby, I wonder who he could be, and it dawns on me that he is the only really enormous person that I have seen in the three weeks that I have been in this country. Almost every person I have seen, male or female, is lean and wiry. This man's form is the evidence of his dietary excess. The general population just can't afford to eat enough to get that way.

Chapter opening photograph: Incense drying in the sun

七

Chapter 8

TODAY IS NEW YEAR'S EVE DAY. We have awakened to find sunshine flowing down from the skies. Although the mud hasn't had a chance to dry out, and I decide that today is the day that I want to see the emperors' tombs. Tin meets me at the dining room of the Binh Minh at 9 a.m, and he, Katherine and I head out. There is no such thing as a car seat in Vietnam…at least where we've been, so she lap-sits.

"Don't get used to this, young lady," I tell her. "Mommy could get in BIG trouble for this back home!" Not that there's anywhere that we're going very fast, and even if we *did* hit something, or vice versa, we'd probably be the bigger vehicle. I think we'd win.

We start out by crossing the river, and head up the north side of it. Thien Mu pagoda is a short ride upriver. This was the home of the monk Thich Quang Duc, the monk who burned himself alive in 1963 in front of the world media to protest the excesses of then-President Diem's regime and the oppression of Buddhists. Tin offers to watch Katherine while I view the pagoda, and after a moment I agree that it's a good idea. There are many steps, he says.

No kidding. After the short walk up the road, I come to the base of a very long, very steep flight of stone steps that rises to the temple on a peak overlooking a bend in the river. The view is as breathtaking as the climb, and I get the chance to appreciate it after I reach the top and lean against a pillar, winded. There are gardens in front, and the temple has an outer and inner chamber, the inner chamber containing the statue of the Buddha. There is the usual offering box, and when money is placed in it, a monk strikes the large brass bell.

Those who bow to the Buddha do not bow to a god or deity. They bow out of respect to a mortal man who figured it out, who became enlightened, who realized one day why everything is the way that it is. Why there is suffering in the world. Why we grow old, get sick and die. He realized the cycle of all that is, and that everything is as it should be. In doing so, he attained peace, and decided that he would show others the way, the path, to reach the same enlightenment. The *Dharma* is that path. He believed that every one of us already has the capacity to be enlightened, we each have that seed inside of us. *Thay* says it is our Buddha-nature. When we bow to the Buddha, or to any other human being, we are bowing towards their Buddha nature, and acknowledging our own at the same time. None of us is bigger or smaller or more or less important than any other person.

I place my dollar in the slot in the wooden box, and bow. My hands are placed palms together in front of me. I lift them to lightly touch my forehead, then to my sternum, over my heart, then I sit down on my heels, and bend forward at the waist until my forehead touches the floor. In this folded position, I take a deep, slow, relaxing breath, then rise to my feet. There are some older Vietnamese women to the left of me who watch curiously, Westerner that I am. All of the other Caucasians climb the steps with their guidebook in hand because it tells them they should come here. They peek around and leave again, able to check one more site off of their list. The monk who rang the gong comes up to me and hands me a laminated card with a picture of the Buddha and Quan Am on the front, and both Chinese and Vietnamese writing on the back. Receiving it, I hold it in my hand, smile and bow. He does the same. We exchange no words, yet we are sharing something that needs no words.

Back down in the parking lot, I find Tin chatting with some women at one of the souvenir booths. Katherine is sitting on one of their laps, happily eating a banana. The women fawn over her. When she sees me walk up, the banana and everyone else are forgotten, as she practically leaps out to be lifted up in my arms. When I pick her up, she now gives me a little squeeze of excitement with her whole body. It's delicious.

ONE BY ONE, Tin takes me on the official Royal Mausoleum Tour. We start with Minh Mang's, where I have to take a ferry across the river. Then comes Khai Dinh's, then Tu Duc's. On the ferry back from Minh Mang, I see something very tall and white on a distant mountain. A column of sorts? Definitely man-made. I point to another passenger, and they can't even see it. When I get back to the far shore, I can't ask Tin because now it's out of view.

Katherine is, once again, sitting in the lap of a woman who is under an awning selling fruit. Tin is leaning against the car chatting with her. Katherine is happily eating mangosteens, little purple-red fruit with a white fleshy interior and large black seeds. I've never had one before, but she is obviously enjoying them. I don't have much choice but to buy some from the woman (fee for babysitting service), and the moment I purchase this small bag, all of the children hanging around pounce on me with their stacks of postcards. "Madam! Madam!" No. No, I have, I have... "Do you have a quarter? Please! Madam! Madam!"

The mangosteens are tart and sweet at the same time. I polish off a handful, spitting the seeds out into the tall grass. Soon we are bumping out down the narrow dirt road. After about twenty minutes, we round a curve and to the right of us, on top of a mountain, there is a HUGE statue of a robed woman on top. Ah! The white column! I ask Tin if it is Quan Am, the female Bodhisattva of Compassion. He said yes, and we immediately pass a sign that says, basically, "Quan The Am this way." ('the' is pronounced 'tay')

Quan The Am! That is one of the chants we learned in Plum Village! It has a haunting melody that stuck with me after just hearing it once. When I hummed the tune to one of the nuns later, she told me what it was and that I could find the words written down in the Plum Village Song and Chant book. *"Namo Botat Quan The Am,"* I begin singing to Katherine. All it consists of are those words repeating themselves as the tune changes, then it starts all over again. Tin spins around, a very surprised look on his face.

"How do you know *Namo Botat?"* I tell him from *Thay.*

> Subj: Haggling with a nun
> Date: 1/2/02 4:36:07 PM
> From: Efitz
> To: Vietnam Group
> *Sent from the Internet (Details)*

> Greetings everyone!

> I'm happy to say that we have finally had some wonderful days of sunshine in Hue, and we have seen the sights a little bit. We have spent a lot of our time at the school our Norfolk group built. It is administered by a pagoda of Buddhist nuns that are affiliated with Thich Nhat Hanh. *Thay,* we call him, which means 'teacher.' Katherine has been surrounded by shaved heads, and they love having her around. The head abbess, sister Minh Thanh, calls herself grandma!

> I received pledges for donations to the school totaling $355 so far, so we went shopping for the kids — one Caucasian (me), an American-Vietnamese friend named Christine, for translation, one of the Vietnamese teachers, and a Buddhist nun in robes, shaved head and straw hat. We bought clothes, coats

and book bags for 35 children, with a discount for bulk buying, and the best price for having a nun along. I bought some silk to have a couple of dresses made, and received local-person price instead of tourist price...the man said that he couldn't lie with a nun there! 22,000 *dong* per meter (remember: 15,000 *dong* is $1 US). So there we were on two motorbikes, four people and three garbage bags full of clothes held between us and our legs, dodging cars, people, bikes and cyclos, and....the nun was the first one back to the hotel. Again. The moral of this story is: never underestimate a nun!

I also had time to spend at Thich Nhat Hanh's pagoda (we call him *Thay*, which means teacher) a few nights ago while friends watched Katherine. It was a wonderful experience to be able to sit and meditate and listen to the chanting of a temple full of orange-robed monks one evening as the rain was falling outside. The monk who translated for us, Tu Niem, said he was so touched by my story of coming to Vietnam to adopt Katherine that instead of meditating, he pulled out some paper and wrote us a poem. He's translating it into English, and I can't wait to read it. What a special gift!

We were supposed to head back to Hanoi in a few days, but I e-mailed the attorney, and her paperwork won't be ready. So I postponed our flight another week, and will visit a little more in Hue. At the nun's pagoda, I watched them make incense from scratch, taking ground sandalwood powder, adding water to make a paste, then rolling it into a thin snake around a bamboo stick. Then it is dried in the sunshine. Always wanted to know how they did that! The woman who makes the incense makes 10,000 *dong* a day doing this...

Some more cost insights: dinner the other night with Allen, him having a large fruit salad, me having tofu with vegetables with steamed rice and two lemonades: 22,000 *dong*. Grilled shrimp is a splurge at 18,000 *dong*. Katherine's little shoes: 8,000 dong. My very nice hotel room is $17 a night. Cafe *sua* (excellent coffee with sweetened condensed milk): 4,000 *dong*. I'll let you guys do the math. After buying that great red and black silk for nun's price ;), then having a long dress hand-tailored, about $12 total.

My driver, Tin, took us today to some tombs of the emperors. Katherine knows him from other days, so she likes to stay with him while I roam around. I asked Tin about what he thinks about us having an attitude about eating dog meat. He said that many westerners like to try dog meat here so they can say that they did it (yuk!). He also said not all Vietnamese eat dog meat. Strict Buddhists eat no meat at all. Not-so-strict Buddhists only eat cow and pig and chicken. SO guys, according to Tin, it's only the CATHOLICS who eat dog. Swear to god (or Buddha, whatever), that's what he said! Special catholic dog meat market in the morning!

Well, I'm sure I've forgotten to list some things. Last time I meant to tell everyone about the first time I used the "M" word...mommy. We were in Hanoi one night, and I had to say to Katherine "No No! This is MOMMY'S pizza!" :) Now she wants to eat everything that she sees me eating! She continues to be a joy, and occasionally lets me sleep for more than 2 hours at a time.

Take care everyone, and I hope that everyone's holidays were wonderful!

Love, Ellen

I AM NOT DISAPPOINTED TO STAY HERE in Hue a few days longer. Still much to see and do now that the rain has eased up, and it's so wonderful to be among friends. Besides, it's cheaper to stay here, and Katherine and I keep the hotel housekeeping staff amused with our crawling races in the hallway. That's *one* way to get her to burn some calories and to tire her out!

She's not yet walking at almost fourteen months. The first few days that she was with me, she didn't squirm around much, and would pretty much stay where I put her. I realized that this was due to delayed muscle development. I doubt that she has spent much time out of her crib for the past seven months. I could tell that she was attached to her caregiver that day in the orphanage director's office, and that her caregiver returned the sentiment, but there are only so many workers to go around for many children. Regular exercise for little ones is probably not a priority. But over the past few weeks, she has gone from just being able to sit up and move in the little bit of the space around her to becoming a first-class speed demon on all fours. Being confined to such a small space for so long, it probably didn't even occur to her that she could keep moving in a straight line for more than a foot or so. She has caught on quickly.

We are back at Long Tho pagoda. When I first arrive, Christine calls out to make sure all the nuns know that I am here. They come from all different corners of the grounds. It is time for their adjustments! One morning a few days ago, one of the Sisters wasn't able to come out and join us when we arrived. We were told that she was laying down with a headache. I asked Christine to go tell her that I am a Chiropractor, to explain to her what a Chiropractor was, and that I would be happy to work on her if she liked. My patient came out of her room and we found a spot in one of the spare sleeping rooms. There was a hard wooden bed on which we spread a blanket. In a pinch, I have worked on people before on picnic table benches, floors, Buddhist library tables. If somebody's hurting and I can do something about it, I sure will try if they want me to.

Checking out the alignment of her neck by feeling how it moved and rotated, I felt some issues in the vertebrae and muscles that could easily cause a headache. I told her (through Christine) what an adjustment was, and what she was going to feel, then did my thing. She started giggling. That's it, I told her, and helped her rise. She smiled, continuing to giggle, then bowed to me. I bowed back. You're welcome.

Her headache *did* go away, within minutes in fact, and now, when I show up, the Sisters line up for their treatments. I see it as my contribution, a way of helping them out for all of the hard work that they do at the school. The nuns who don't work at the school especially need help, as they tend to the pagoda's rice paddies, which is back-breaking work. All day long bending and stooping and twisting, carrying heavy loads, and wading through water and mud. Christine says that they hate the leeches the most. They attach themselves onto the nuns' legs and bite and suck until they draw blood, making the Sisters shriek and jump up onto the built-up levy to yank it off. You can never see them coming in the muddy water…

Once my makeshift office is empty of patients, we head over to the school. Today is the day that we will distribute the clothes and supplies to the children. In the conference room, the Sisters and teachers have labeled each package with a child's name, and the packages are then bagged according to classroom. At the first classroom, as each package is drawn out, Sister Minh Thanh reads the name on it, and the child comes forward to claim their gift. I have brought Katherine with me today, and she rides my hip as I hand each package to the children. When they receive it, they give a little bow and say 'cam on,' thank you, and return to their seat to patiently wait while the others get their turn. "*Cam on*," I answer back, returning their bow with my one free hand.

When all the gifts have been given out, the teachers let the children loose. It looks like Christmas as they tear into the plastic wrapping. Everything is immediately tried on, whether it is coat, dress, shirt, trousers or pajamas. Most put the items on right over the clothes they have on. A few of the boys strip down right there, so they can put on their fancy new duds. I help with buttons here, a zipper there…the clothes have 'brand new' creases in them, 'brand new' smell, 'brand new' crispness. A boy who had trouble with his zipper has tucked his dress shirt into his trousers and is tugging on my sleeve. I turn, and see him standing there with his bare feet sticking out from the bottom of his pants legs. His shirt is buttoned all the way up to the top, and he has such a smile on his face. He is so proud.

We repeat the routine in the other three classrooms, and except for one girl who is upset that she got a jacket, but she likes the blue polka-dotted dress that a friend got better, there are lots of happy smiles and excited faces. When we return to the conference room with the empty bags, I see one more pile of clothes on the table. But we've been to all of the classrooms. Were some of the children not here today?

"Those are for the children who are unable to come to the school…their disabilities prevent them from traveling, so a teacher goes each week to their homes to work with them there," Christine tells me. I ask if the teacher will bring them on her next trip. "*You* should go today," she said. "You are the giver, you should pass them out yourself."

Arrangements are made for Phuong's mother Kim to take me by motorbike to the remaining five houses. Katherine will stay at the pagoda with the nuns. They will even feed her dinner, her new favorite, rice soup with vegetables.

The rain has returned. Kim doesn't speak any English, but that does nothing to stop her from enthusiastically chatting to me along the way over her shoulder. Even if I could understand her, I still wouldn't be able to hear her over the flapping of my poncho hood in the wind as we travel down the narrowing dirt, well, dirt and mud, roads.

Christine follows us with Phuong on the other motorbike. There are no cars this far away from the city. These people could never afford them. We pass bicycles and motorbikes and a lot of people on foot. I see the water-buffalo out in the fields to the left and right of us as we drive along. Bodies (it's hard to tell men from women, as they both wear the same tunic, pants and straw hats) stand knee-deep in water, bending and straightening, bending and straightening. We turn off the main road to the left and are now on a well-packed path that is wider than a sidewalk, but narrower than a road. Just wide enough for two motorbikes, or water-buffalo, to pass each other. It is kind of like suburbia, Vietnam style, with branches off this artery leading to residential areas of roughly built structures. Each time there is a branch, the path gets narrower and narrower.

We make our last turn, and Kim pulls up a slope into a dirt yard. Phuong and Christine are right behind us. There is a fenced area containing chickens and pigeons. A dog barks. The house is made of cinderblock, with door openings and window openings, but no doors or windows in those openings. A young girl about eight years old stands in front of the house. There is no one else around. Kim calls out to her, and the girl points to the house. She follows us in. There are a few plain pieces of wooden furniture, but when I look to the left I freeze. There is a low wooden plank-top table, about five feet by five feet. No sheet or covers, padding or pillows, just bare wood. On it is a boy, I would guess him to be ten, maybe more. His head is towards us, twisted in an odd way, and he looks at us. He has Cerebral Palsy, Christine tells me, which has contorted his body so severely that at first I can't tell if he is lying on his stomach or back. His arms and legs are twisted and mangled-looking, elbows up, wrists cocked and down, fingers and feet twisted.

Christine exchanges a few words with Phuong. "Their parents are in the fields, working with the rice. They are there from sunup to sundown. The children are here all day like this, by themselves. The parents have no way to get the little girl to school, and there is nothing else that they can do for their son, other than feed him, bathe him."

When the boy moves, it is more like flopping around, not very controlled. He probably has learned over the years to not get too close to the edge. We have brought him two pairs of pajamas, and I go over to the bed, lean over, touch him on the shoulder (yes, now I can tell that he is lying on his back), and place the packages next to him on his platform. His muscles twitch and he is unable to keep looking at me. He is incapable of reaching for the clothes himself, but he makes some excited high-pitched noises. They don't need to translate anything for me.

Allen has told me that a certain percentage of children with Cerebral Palsy have normal or near-normal intelligence, but they are trapped in an uncontrollable, degenerating body. Our school, *L'Ecole de L'Aimee* means School of the Beloved, but this is a play on words. The school is named after Allen's sister, Aimee, who was born with Cerebral Palsy. In French, Aimee means the name Amy as well as 'beloved.' I look at this boy, and can't even imagine what his life must be like, here in this one-room house, living each and every day on this platform.

OUR NEXT VISITS are much the same, long drives down roads that turn into paths that turn into trails, that sometimes even just disappear into leaves and mulch. Then we see a cinderblock house, a tin roof perhaps. A couple of times we get lost, and Kim has to stop to ask directions from people walking down the paths, or sitting together at intersections at makeshift shacks sharing tea and conversation. Always we are waved on, sending us further and further into the remote countryside of Vietnam. I catch the curious looks from those seeing the white face and tall nose peeking out from over Kim's shoulder.

At each house, no matter how humble—really, they are all humble—I am offered a stool to sit on, a cup of tea, shy smiles and bows. At one, a child in a bed suffers from obvious retardation. In another, a grinning little boy lurches towards me on legs twisted and thin as sticks. The other siblings come close, hovering near to me, and are sometimes brave enough to touch my sleeve, my pants leg, or hang onto my fingers for a moment. I smile back and wish that I had brought along some of the candy that I bought at the market.

As we travel from house to house, I think of how different this is from the Vietnam of thirty years ago that I know from the movies. Around me, the trees and foliage are lush and green and vibrant. The fields flow one into another into another. It is quite beautiful. It is hard to believe that this, and other parts of the country, were bombed into a moonscape not so long ago. Where man's hand has carved and gouged the land, time and the gentle but determined force of nature have softened and absorbed without grudge or grief.

I remember to take a long, slow deep breath in. In spite of what I see when we visit the houses of these children, I somehow can still see the beauty of the countryside around me. Beauty and horror. Beauty and horror. Somehow the two manage to exist in the same place at the same time.

THE DAY BEFORE WE LEAVE for Hanoi, we are at Long Tho pagoda and Christine comes up to us.

"Do you want to meet Grandmother nun?"

Grandmother nun, a literal translation of her title, *Su Ba*, is the head of the lineage of Sister Minh Thanh's order. They share their Buddhist tradition with the monks of Tu Hieu, and the nun's pagoda is, in fact, right next door to them. She is 95 years old and often isn't at this location. "It is a rare opportunity," she tells us.

On the ride over, I tell Christine to ask if the *Su Ba* would like to tell stories of the old days, or whatever she would like, and I would tape them on my camcorder. That way the stories could be saved. She will ask, she tells me.

WHEN THE FAMILIAR ARCHES and tranquil pond of Tu Hieu come into view, I ask if I can stop for a short visit with Tu Niem and the Abbot for my promised introduction of Katherine. I retrace my footsteps of the other day, around the pond, through the leaves and pine needles of the forest floor, then up to the main terrace. I carry Katherine on my hip.

Word must have spread about our unannounced arrival, because Tu Niem appears a few minutes later, smiling his broad smile.

"So this is the baby!" he says. "Huong!" he addresses Katherine.

"She was asking about her poem," I tease him.

"Ah, yes, I have brought it with me." He draws out a piece of paper from within the folds of his robe. As he passes it to me, I use my left arm to send Katherine his way. She reaches out to grab onto his shoulder, her gaze never leaving his bushy eyebrows.

She is content for the moment, so I carefully unfold the paper to read his precise script.

To Ellen and Huong from Tu Niem
From the West,
You came here.
To my country
From a cold winter.
Unfolded your hands and opened your heart,
Like a spring presence in the middle of winter.
You begin to touch Huong's life, to season
her life with sweetness,
To brighten the life of a newborn.
A newborn, who like a wild flower,
was cast to the side of the road,
Then stepped on.
Filled with emotion, I stood and stared as you left.
Soon you will return to the west,
and your golden image will always be printed in my heart.

I LOOK UP TO WATCH the young, gentle man, this poet, bounce my child up and down, smiling into her face with open affection. He holds her as if there is nothing else in the world that he would rather be doing right now.

I share his sentiment.

WHEN WE REACH THE NUN'S PAGODA, as usual there is a feast waiting for us. Whenever we arrive at the pagodas, we are treated to a feast of vegetarian foods. Again I see before me dumplings, soups, salads, noodles and rice, tofu and vegetables, and lots of fresh fruit. I have had several different types of bananas, all of them short and stubby, but with very intense flavor…slightly citrus-y. Then there is a fruit called *sampuchea* that I love. It looks like an Asian pear, but has a sweet honey taste like nothing I know. The first time I had it was in one of my hotels when they left a fruit basket in my room. I ate the fruit, then ran with the peel to the housekeeping staff so they could write down the name for me. Then there is, what Christine tells me translates as "Breast Milk Fruit." A green-ish, purple-ish, shiny-skinned fruit about the size of a peach that you cut in half, remove the large black seeds, then scoop out the white gelatinous pulp with a spoon. It is very sweet, and it oozes a thin white juice that looks, well, like breast milk. Katherine shares just about everything with me, but usually one of the nuns whisks her off to feed her veggie and rice soup. Christine tells me that the younger nuns almost fight over this job!

Once again, I am stuffed. Christine comes over and tells me that yes, the Su Ba will talk for the video. I go get the camcorder out of my backpack, and she leads me to a room that is in the rear of the temple. While we are setting up, the monks from Tu Hieu have come by and begin chanting in the inner chamber in the front. They chant rhythmically to the beat of a small bell and a wooden block.

The Su Ba is ready, and Christine, Sister Minh Thanh and I are sitting around her. Christine holds the camera first. The Su Ba starts to talk, and the monks continue to chant behind us. I don't, of course, understand anything that she is saying, but I sit and smile and breathe and think about how lucky I am to be right here, right now, in this place, sharing this moment. Some people go through their whole lives and never experience a moment such as this, this intimate glimpse into another culture, of lives so different from our own. Yet again I am overwhelmed by a feeling of gratitude to be allowed into the lives of these people. And I wouldn't be here if it weren't for Katherine. Katherine has given this adventure to me. At the moment she is still with the novice nuns, but I know that she would love to be watching the Su Ba, and listening to the bells and chanting.

From time to time, Christine whispers to me a translation of what the Su Ba is talking about. Being a young nun in the old days with nothing to eat, and building this place piece by piece by hand. How Vietnam has changed. How the people have changed, as have the lives of the monks and nuns. We tape for almost an hour. Christine and I switch off on holding the camera and back again, and one of the nuns eventually brings Katherine to me.

The Su Ba pauses, then turns to us, begins talking again, then pauses again. Christine turns to me. The Su Ba is watching Katherine.

"She is telling me about your daughter." She says. "She says that the two of you are together because of your *duyen phan*." Now its Christine's turn to pause. I can tell that she is struggling to translate what this term means. "*Duyen phan* (pronounced like 'jwen-fun') means sort of like destiny and karma and fate all rolled into one. It is your destiny, how it was meant to be, that you are together."

"Did you tell the *Su Ba* about how I had the picture of the other child, and how, on the day I went to the orphanage, they told me she wasn't mine, and they brought me Katherine?" I asked her. I had ended up telling Allen and Christine the story of what happened that day. I still have not looked back, but I continue to wonder what other peoples' reactions would be. Allen had dismissed it, turning to Katherine sitting in her stroller, and saying how absolutely beautiful she is. End of discussion, as far as he was concerned.

"Yes, she knows that," Christine says. Apparently it has been a topic of conversation amongst the nuns as well.

The *Su Ba* began speaking again, and we waited for her to pause. "She says that because of your *duyen phan* what happened that day is precisely what was supposed to happen. You ended up with the child that you were meant to have. You were meant to be together in this lifetime, and you have come all the way to Vietnam so you would be together. If she had been born somewhere else in the world, it may have been now, or it may have been later, but your paths would have crossed."

Reincarnation is a given concept in Buddhism. Everyone knows that we have all been here before many times, and that we will all be returning many times. It is a continuing cycle, and only when we become enlightened do we have the opportunity to break free of it. In the meantime, hopefully with each turn around we become a better, wiser, more compassionate person, learning the lessons that we have to learn...and being with the people who will help us on this journey.

I look at Katherine folded in my arms on my lap, feeling her warm body sheltered by mine. Some of the e-mails from home have asked me, "Can you believe that you love someone so much? Aren't you just consumed by your love for that child?"

Really, I can't say so. I have love for this child, and I fall in love with her more each day. She enchants me, makes me laugh, she even makes my gut twist when we look in each others' eyes. But I don't feel possessive of her, I don't feel consumed. She is not MINE in that sense. I feel more like a nurturer, responsible for her, taking care of her, teaching her, guiding her, loving her, as she grows into the adult human being that she will be. Along the way we will bring each other joys and sorrows and so many other things.

My real gut feeling is that she has been around the block a few more times than I have, and somehow she has chosen this time to go around it with me. There is no doubt in my mind that it will be an interesting journey. I am sure that in the end, I have just as much to learn from her as she does from me.

The *Su Ba* motions for me to come a little closer. I scoot my stool forward. Katherine sits on my lap watching her. The *Su Ba* says some words to her in Vietnamese, interspersed with a "hmmm-mm?" here and a "hmmmmmm?" there. During the past hour that she has been talking, she had held her beads in her hand, a string of white Buddhist prayer beads. She now lifts her arm and holds them out, swinging them in front of Katherine. A few more words in Vietnamese, another "hmmmmm?"

Christine whispers in my direction. "Tibetan," she said. "She is testing her."

Katherine sits still in my lap, watching the beads swing back and forth like a pendulum.

"She's not reaching for them," Christine whispers.

Fidgety, curious Katherine not reaching for something so tantalizing, just within reach? Impossible! The *Su Ba* swings them enticingly closer. Forward and back, right and left. Katherine still doesn't bite.

"What's she doing?" I ask Christine.

"If she doesn't reach for the beads, she's not going to be a nun…"

The *Su Ba* starts to chuckle, as does Sister Minh Thanh sitting by her side. They exchange a few words together.

"She's not going to be a nun," Christine says. "She will be a lay practitioner like her mother. That is what she says."

So the bead thing was the nun test…interesting. She's not going to be a nun. In this culture, being a nun is a positive thing, good for the family's fortune, and a person is guaranteed that they won't go hungry for the rest of their life. But for me, becoming a nun is not high on my list of what I envision my little girl growing into! Well, OK, if she grows up and wants to be a nun, I will support her whatever is to be for her this time around. We will see.

"Cam on," I tell the *Su Ba.* Thank you. I place Katherine's palms together between my two hands, and she and I bow toward the *Su Ba* together. She and Sister Minh Thanh bow back. Our audience is over.

Chapter opening photograph: Katherine with the poet/monk, Tu Niem

八

Chapter 9

I SHOULD HAVE STAYED in Hue! I came all the way back to Hanoi only to find out that the province won't be finished processing my papers until next week. I have enjoyed this city. The people are friendly, and it is always interesting to walk around, no matter how many times I've covered the same ground. It has become familiar. But the noise and traffic! They are a serious challenge to my Buddhist state of mind.

I will *not* stay around here for another whole week. I briefly consider flying back down to Hue. The airfare is only around $66. But I'm also tempted to do something different while I have the time and the chance.

On yet another tour around old town, I pop into an Internet café/travel office. Katherine is, as usual, in her stroller, and within minutes, as usual, she starts to squirm. The girls running the shop are more than happy to entertain her as a diversion to their uneventful day. One of the girls stands by the door with Katherine on her hip, watching the traffic and pedestrians go by. Fresh pastries appear from the shop next door. We hear a steady 'boom! boom!' that gets louder and louder. It is a funeral procession. In the lead is a brightly decorated cart being pulled by a donkey. The opening at the back of the cart is draped with sheer fabric, and inside you can see a casket. Walking behind is row upon row of mourners. They step slowly to the beat of a large drum that is balanced on the belly of a stoic-faced older man in formal garb who follows in the rear. Both the cart and the clothing of the mourners are a rainbow of brilliant colors, so different from the somber black of funerals at home. It's as if those left behind are wishing the loved one a glorious departure. Perhaps it is because here, death is seen as just a segue into the spirit life, one where the departed is now a respected and valued ancestor. Their spirit will linger on to watch over generations to come, and be prayed for and remembered by those generations, and, eventually, be born again.

Business stops on the street as the procession files by, and everyone turns to watch. Inside the shop, an Asian man makes a comment about the loveliness of the flowers and decorations on the cart in very good English. When I reply we begin chatting, and it turns out that he is from Hong Kong, but lives in New York City.

"New York! That's where I was born!"

We chat and compare notes on some of the Dim Sum restaurants on Mott Street, and then about our impressions of Hanoi. He is here trying to expand his business in import/export...export form Vietnam, of course. Soon conversation turns to Katherine.

"She is your daughter," he says, more of a statement than a question.

"Yes." And I tell him the abbreviated version of the story about traveling to Vietnam to adopt her. While we speak, we watch her play and giggle and laugh with the girls at the front of the shop. Over these few weeks together, she has gotten a glow, a sparkle that I attribute to good nourishment and unlimited adored attention.

"She has so much good energy about her," my new friend says.

"Yes, she does," I agree. "Good food and loving attention do wonders."

"Yes, that," he replied, "but she has good energy about her because you have good energy about you."

"Ah!" I said, understanding now. "Good chi!" Chi is Chinese for vital life force, the energy of your body and spirit. What they would have said in the sixties would have been: "man, you've got good vibes." That's chi. I picked that up on my esoteric journeys over these past eight years or so.

"Oh, you know chi?" he said. "Yes! She has good chi because you have good chi."

"Yes, I think she sucks it out of me during the night when we snuggle," I say, only half-joking.

"That is what babies do," he replied. "When they aren't strong enough to generate much of their own chi, they get it from you. She hasn't gotten any chi from anyone for a long time, so she has some catching up to do."

I laugh. "Yep, that's me. I've got the chi, she sucks it out!"

Our friend gathers his things to leave. "Perhaps we will bump into each other again here. It has been nice talking with you," he says. He pays for his computer usage, then chats a little to Katherine on his way out the door. She flirts shamelessly with him, batting her eyes, and reaching out from the girl's arms towards him, only to pull them back when he reaches out for her.

At the desk I inquire about the trips that they schedule. I would like to find a three day or so trip to take. One of the places I had planned on hitting when I thought that I would be solo was Sa Pa, a town in the mountains west of Hanoi. In Sa Pa there is a concentration of several of the ethnic minorities, and many of them live much as they did hundreds of years ago. They have their own style of dress, of building houses, of community and of supporting themselves. I have spoken to a few people, however, and the consensus is that it would probably be a little rugged for a baby. Plus, it is an overnight train ride to get there, which also has the reputation for lack of comfort.

My other option is to go to the coast...to Ha Long Bay. The books say that this area of Vietnam has some of the most dramatic topography in the world. A part of the film *Indochine* was filmed there, and the views I remember are haunting. With an undergrad minor in Geology under my belt, I've got a soft spot for rocks, even if I can't pick out a plagioclaise feldspar from a schist anymore.

It turns out that Sinh Café has tours that leave every morning for Ha Long Bay, and I can stay as many days as I like. There is a 2 ½ hour bus ride to Haiphong, then an additional 2 hour ferry-boat ride to Cat Ba island where the hotel is. Half of Cat Ba island is a National Park, and although the main attraction is hiking, I won't be doing much of that. I just want to get away to a slower pace and see something new. Cat Ba is going to be it.

The whole package is a great deal. Katherine and I get all of our transportation, plus dinners and breakfasts, and three nights lodging for $35. That's what I'm paying for one night at the good ol' Army Guesthouse! If I leave tomorrow, that will only leave us a couple of days once we get back before the official adoption up in Lang Son. Perfect!

When my gaze returns to the front of the shop, Katherine is being bounced up and down frenetically by one of the girls who is repeating something over and over to her in Vietnamese. Katherine's glow has been replaced by a shade of blue, she has tears in her blinking eyes, and her fingers are in her silent mouth. She is choking.

I don't recall the steps that carry me to her side, but in the next second I am snatching her away from the girl, thrusting her belly-down over my left hand and giving her several sharp *thwaks*! on the back with my right palm. On the second blow, a wad of soft, white, partially-chewed bread pops out of her mouth and onto the floor. Lifting her face back to mine, I gaze at her watery eyes and see her take in a raspy breath before she lets out a weak wail. The girls have gathered around me, chattering excitedly, but none of them act terribly upset or worried. Jesus Christ, I think...how many babies die in this country because they don't know anything equivalent to the Heimlich Maneuver!?

A small baguette rests innocently on the table near us with the soft middle pulled out from the hard crusty shell. As I comfort and hug Katherine's tiny body close to mine, the enormity of my responsibility is hammered home that much more. I am never, never, ever off duty, waking or sleeping, with her in my presence or not, with my back turned for a millisecond or with her in my arms with her face inches from mine. Any one of a million things can happen at any moment, and a portion of my brain is now allocated to always having her presence and safety in its consciousness. Today, tomorrow and for the rest of my life.

An hour later, I watch Katherine's sleeping body. Her back rises and falls rhythmically, softly, as she lies like a little snail, belly-down on my bed. Her breath gushes through barely-parted lips. Breath and life. So fragile. I breathe with her, my ribcage expanding and contracting in unison with hers. I watch, fascinated and absorbed, and the rest of the world falls away, for minutes, for hours. The present moment expands and envelops us, defying counting or measurement.

THE AFTERNOON SUNSHINE FALLS on my head and shoulders as I push Katherine's stroller down Hai Ba Trung. I have the awning open, shading her from the bright rays. There is one more sight I want to see before leaving tomorrow.

We turn left on Pho Hoa Lo and walk along a sidewalk edged by a long, high wall. In several places, there are crumbling cracks where time is trying to break through, although there are no actual holes yet. Eventually we stop at an arched opening. There is a sign in Vietnamese above. This is Hoa Lo prison, the infamous 'Hanoi Hilton.' American Air Force and Navy fliers were imprisoned here during the war, including Senator John McCain, who spent five years within these walls.

I enter a stone building, lifting Katherine's stroller up and over a raised concrete threshold. At the desk I pay the several thousand-

dong entry fee and receive an orange brochure that is printed in Vietnamese, French and English. Much of the prison, built around 1900 by the French, was demolished to make way for the two soaring structures next door, the Hanoi Towers. What remains is a museum dedicated primarily to the Vietnamese revolutionaries imprisoned as a result of their quest for freedom from France years before America even became involved here.

As I push Katherine's stroller from one cold, bare room to the next, small plaques identify iron shackles, implements of torture, and even a guillotine that the French used for executions. I peer into rooms through tiny barred windows to see stone slabs with chains and locks attached to immobilize their occupants. A tiny metal door covers a slit through which food must have been passed. Even without relying on the government-produced information in my hand and posted in the rooms, the damp walls of this place scream *misery*.

At the very end of the maze of rooms and corridors, we come to an open-air courtyard. Propped against one wall is a volleyball net, the knots and string dark with age. A sign tells me that it was used for exercise by the American aggressors imprisoned here. A building to the left houses a series of photographs of the Americans receiving letters and writing home, and standing together in groups. The captions state and restate how well the Americans were treated during their stay. The reality that the government has decided to perpetuate. Bits and pieces that I have heard through the media over the years from these men who wryly gave this place the nickname 'Hanoi Hilton' say otherwise.

Walking on this land for the past five weeks, I feel as if I am treading on many lands all at once, each somehow co-existing yet completely separate from the other. There are the friendly and curious people that I meet each day, beautiful cities and countryside, luscious fruit. In my mind I carry the images of the few war movies that I have seen, as well as the pain of friends who lost sons or brothers in the war. Of shared confidences from veterans who confess to having killed Vietnamese women and children, because they were just as capable of being the enemy, and therefore as deadly, as men. Of the memory of a Vietnamese-American friend who recalls wandering through a field at dusk in the Mekong Delta in the 1980's, and swears that she felt the grasping presence of lingering American souls trying to reach out to her, their ghostly fingertips brushing her shoulders. Of the stories of the people from the Vietnam Babylift, who I met through my connections on the APV, when hundreds of orphans were rescued when Saigon fell in 1975. Then there is the omnipresent specter of the government, sometimes not noticed at all for days on end, then, when reading a brochure or dealing with officials, or taking care of some other formality, there is the unspoken but felt *don't say the wrong thing, don't do the wrong thing, don't take a photograph here…*

I pass back through the arched entranceway and turn left on Pho Hoa Lo to head back to the hotel. There is a brisk wind in our faces, and this side of the street now falls in the shadows of the walls and buildings. There really wasn't much to interest Katherine at the prison, although she was quiet enough as long I kept up the pace. A man walking towards us begins speaking quickly and urgently to me in Vietnamese, eventually admonishing me, although I can't understand a word that he says. Finally he motions with his hands for me to turn the stroller around and go the other way. He wants me to walk in the other direction so the wind won't be in Katherine's face.

THAT EVENING, Katherine and I return to the banks of Hoan Kiem Lake to dine at a restaurant that caters to tourists. The outdoor café is where Katherine and I shared our first ice cream. In the evenings, they have live traditional Vietnamese music, and the windows look out upon the shining lights of Old Town reflecting off of the lake's surface. We share spring rolls, veggies, tofu, chicken and steamed rice. I have strategically placed Katherine's stroller so she gets to watch the show.

Two seated women play stringed instruments that look like an autoharp. One woman uses small padded mallets to strike the strings, the other plucks hers with claw-like picks that she wears on the tip of her thumb and first two fingers of her right hand. A third woman strikes a wooden block for percussion. A man plays a wooden flute. They wear brightly colored silk jackets that button up to a high collar, with long narrow sleeves.

Katherine is so entranced with the performance that she has to be coaxed to eat. The musical notes glide up and down, reminding me of the sound of water trickling over bells or chimes. After a few songs, a woman comes out to dance, drifting smoothly between the tables. Each hand holds two tiny porcelain teacups. One she holds stationary, and the other quivers and strikes the first repeatedly, clapping them together like castanets. She hovers at Katherine's side for a few moments, weaving her hands like a flamenco dancer, clinking the cups in time to the music.

It is close to nine o'clock when we climb into a taxi for the ride to the hotel. Katherine is asleep before the lake is out of sight, which is just as well. We have an early start in the morning.

IT IS STILL EARLY, around nine a.m., by the time we reach the ferry terminal in Haiphong. Katherine has done great so far with the bus ride. We sat next to a young German fellow, with whom Katherine flirted, of course. He was traveling with his wife, who was sitting several rows ahead of us. She would peek around me, reach out and touch him gently, played peek-a-boo with him, then, when she finally fell asleep, stretched out so her feet rested on his leg.

The marina is quite chaotic. Not only are there people coming and going at a furious rate, but there aren't enough boat slips. So boats are tethered together, row after row of them, bobbing, reaching out into the bay. This means that if you want to get to a boat that isn't right at the pier (like ours), you've got to climb over boat after boat to get to the one that you want to get to. While carrying your gear. I have Katherine, a suitcase, and a stroller. Everybody pitches in to help. I have four boats to climb onto, over and around, to get to our transport. There are planks without anything to hold onto to traverse, ropes to wrestle and guard rails to scale. It is a regular aquatic obstacle course with bobbing targets, but after all we've been through so far, it's just another day in the life. My bags and the stroller are passed overhead from person to person. I climb, balance, duck, weave and sidle with Katherine clutched to my side with my left arm.

It's a little easier to get to know our fellow travelers on the boat. A bus really doesn't allow you to communicate to anyone much beyond your own row. Now I can get a good look at our companions. Mostly young backpacker-types. European. Some of them have been traveling in Southeast Asia for several months, or even a year around the world. One couple with a four-year-old little boy. Not one other single lady with a baby...not that that's a surprise.

Once underway, the crew starts to serve us lunch. Noodles, rice, veggies, meat, soup — the usual fare that tends to grace the tables here. Not as good as nun food! When the beverages come around, I decide that it's time for a Tiger beer, and relax for a moment savoring the taste of fizz and hops. With lunch over, I carry Katherine to where most of the other passengers are going. Up to the top deck to stretch out and watch the scenery.

It's as if a mountain range came down to the sea, and nobody told it to stop being mountains. The peaks continue on, poking sheerly and dramatically out of the water. Rocky and raw, dark and gray and beautiful, they continue on mile after mile after mile. There is no surf in this bay off of the China Sea. The water is smooth like a mirror, which contrasts the peaks that much more, reflecting the facades back to themselves in reverse. Up on the top deck it is sunny and the ride is smooth, so I let Katherine crawl around a little bit. She is the unofficial entertainment for the other passengers.

Our German friend comes by with his wife. "I told her that a girl on the bus was flirting with me, so she wanted to see who it was." He enjoys the joke that he has played on his wife.

Katherine catches the eye of a Dutch boy, probably about 20 years old, traveling with his friend. Like most Northern Europeans that I have met on my travels, they speak perfect English and we chat about what there is to do on the island, how their trip has been going, and how much longer they will be traveling. Katherine is glancing at him from the corners of her eyes, smiling and looking away, doing her usual flirt routine. "You'd better stop that young lady!" I tell her, waving my finger in her face. "No boys for you until you are at *least* twenty-one! Boys only want one thing!"

My Dutch friend leans towards her, brandishing his finger the same way. "You listen to your mother," he says. "She's right!"

WHEN WE ARRIVE AT THE SUNFLOWER HOTEL, we find sparse surroundings. No crib, not that I expected one, but at least the bed is against the wall, so I don't have to worry about her rolling out. There isn't much privacy. The rooms have sliding windows that open out into the hallway, and the walls are quite thin. I'm worried that Katherine's crying will probably wake up the whole building. Mommy duty is going to be a little more challenging here. As if it hasn't been already. Actually, it has now been five weeks since Katherine and I have been together. She is wonderful and amazing 97% of the time. She only cries at bedtime, usually, and when she's impatient for a bottle, which she still gets morning and evening. But even that's getting less and less. Crying here, however, would rock the house.

I dump the bags and carry Katherine downstairs. The reception staff are letting me keep the stroller behind the front desk. "Vietnam?" they asked. Yes, Vietnam. Her name is Katherine.

"Ahh! Katherine! *Em be!*" Cluck! Cluck! Katherine caught on to her name just before our third week together. She never had responded to Huong, which made me wonder how often she had heard it.

The hotel is right on the street that edges the harbor of Cat Ba City. The two tips of land that encircle the harbor are more of those stark abrupt peaks, as are the mountains behind the hotel. The city, more of a town in size, is narrowly squeezed along the water's edge, and is lined mostly with casual restaurants, hotels, and a couple of karaoke bars.

Between the street and the water is a concrete walk, sometimes just wide enough for two people to walk abreast, other times it opens up to allow produce and trinket sellers, and metal tables and chairs. Hordes of children roam the waters' edge selling postcards. In fact, you can't go very far without being absolutely pestered. Madam! Madam! You buy postcards? Very cheap! And they start flashing the glossy photographs at you. No, No. OK! They respond. Later! You buy later! They are particularly aggressive here.

The harbor itself is very tranquil. At high tide, the water laps gently against the stone levy. At low tide, the stones along the bottom of the wall are exposed. But it's what is in the harbor itself that is so unusual: a floating village. There are dozens of raft structures tethered, not just at the edges of the harbor, but all the way from one side to the other. On the rafts are tents, wooden structures, clotheslines, stoves, dogs…these are the peoples' homes, and they use bamboo skiffs to get to and from the shore, from other homes. There is even a floating restaurant in the middle of it all. Most of these skiffs are tarred, woven bamboo, steered with oars and sticks, that are of a style that has been in use for hundreds of years. At night the lanterns on the boats burn and blink in the darkness.

Katherine and I watch them from the hall balcony of the Sunflower hotel, and listen to the dogs barking from out over the water.

On our first morning in Cat Ba, we hitch a ride on the bus that carries the hikers to the National Forest. I just want to see the scenery, then we'll ride the bus back again. The landscape of Cat Ba Island consists of soaring peaks and bright green valleys. In the fields I see what I see everywhere in Vietnam: stooping men and women, wearing their *non la* to shade their faces from the sun, and simple cotton shirts and trousers. I have not seen much differentiation of chores between the sexes in this country. The women work as hard as and side by side with the men.

On the road to the forest, the buses pull over. We have a chance to look at some caves, 15,000 *dong* entry fee. I ponder whether I want to bring Katherine into a cave, but finally decide with just a dollar on the line, I'll give it a shot. We hike up a trail, up a flight of tiny, shallow steps honed into the side of the cliff, and enter a vaulted cavern. We are told that this cave system was used as a hospital for the northern troops during the American War. They lead us down carved-out hallways and into large, empty, concrete-floored rooms lit by bare light bulbs. This is where the operations were performed under the most brutal conditions. Up to 90% mortality rate, we are told.

Although it is dank and dark, Katherine does fine being carried along. We are led down another corridor, around a corner, down a long flight of stairs, another corner, then through a low-ceilinged tunnel. Coolness radiates down on our heads from the rock so close above us. We find ourselves at a dead-end, and are told to climb a ladder to view another vaulted cavern. Some of the older folks, unable to handle the ladder, turn around and try to find their way out. I follow. We do indeed exit out into another cave, this one at the back of the mountain from where we went in. There is a ladder down instead of steps to navigate. A stick and twine ladder. Our small group stands to chat awhile, admiring the scenery of the fields below, and I am pondering the feasibility of maneuvering down this ladder with Katherine. My only other option is to return and go back out the front cave. I recall that there weren't too many turns, so I decide to go back solo. Well, me and Katherine.

Back down the tunnel I go, passing the side turn where the large group is, who are still in that vaulted chamber. A woman has taken it upon herself to sing and test the acoustics. Her melody echoes through the caverns, vibrating and resounding off of the walls. It becomes hard to distinguish what direction the singing is coming from; it's as if the walls themselves are emitting the notes.

Apparently the guides must throw some master switch after they leave an area, because the bare bulbs are no longer burning in the rooms that I am passing. I come to a ninety degree angle turn to the left, which I know is followed by a long flight of steps, another ninety degree angle turn to the right at the top, then the first big cave is there. When I make the first turn, I am confronted by darkness. The only light is the little bit filtering from behind me. I try to remember about how many steps this flight of stairs is.

Suddenly, I think of *Thay*. I am remembering one of his talks when he said that we can live in the same house for twenty years, and walk in and out thousands of times, and not be able to say how many steps are to our front door. How unmindfully we live when we can walk up and down those stairs, over and over, and not pay enough attention, ever, to know how many steps there are. True, I've only been down this flight of steps once, but my wondering exactly how many I have to walk to reach the other side has brought his words back to me.

I take the first few steps. No trouble...there is still enough residual light from the corner behind me. But it gets darker and darker with each step. Katherine is in my arms, totally still, totally quiet. The warmth of my body seems to be the only sensory input that she needs to feel at ease. "I'm going where you're going. End of discussion."

I now have to feel for the next steps with my feet…I can't see them. I look back over my shoulder. I can still see the dim rectangle of light at the bottom right end of the stairs. Turning back, the only thing I can see ahead of me is…nothing. I cannot even see my hand held in front of my face, not even after standing still a few moments to let my eyes become more accustomed to the light, or lack thereof. A couple of more steps. I must be past half way. Surely I will start to see a similar dim glow up ahead and to the right where I know the next turn is. Nothing. The singing that had been fading, stops altogether. Now there is no sound. My open eyes pick up not a glimmer of light.

I feel no fear in the darkness. The presence of the mountain surrounds and engulfs me, but it holds for me no animosity. It has been here forever, and those of us who have traveled deep inside its guts have left barely a memory to linger splashed on its walls. Perhaps I am bold because I have to be, with Katherine held tightly in my arms. My logical mind tells me: *this is just a path with a beginning and an end. All you have to do is put one foot in front of the other, and you will end up somewhere. If you can't go back, all you need to do is turn around and trust in the way.*

I pause, weighing in my memory the steps ahead, the steps behind, that twine and stick ladder, the little girl in my arms…and I turn back. I carefully pivot. Somehow, not having a visual reference makes balance a little more difficult. I place my right hand along the wall, and slowly make my way back. One, two, three, four. I breathe and count my way down the flight of stairs. The dim rectangle at the bottom grows brighter and larger. Eleven, twelve, thirteen…I hear faint footsteps, a large clumsy crowd is climbing back down their ladder to make their own way out. Nineteen, twenty, twenty-one…I can now see the steps that I am placing my feet on, and am almost at the corner that I will turn and see the rest of the group. Twenty-seven, twenty-eight. Twenty-eight. I'm down. As I round the corner, I see a few of the group making their way down the hall towards the smaller rear cave. Twenty-eight steps. I want to ask the guide how many steps are in that staircase, to know how close I was, how far I had gone, but somehow, I don't think he'll know either, no matter how many times he's been down them.

THAT STICK AND TWINE LADDER ended up not being much worse than climbing over the four boats in Haiphong. By the side of the road, an entrepreneur has brought up fruit to sell to us tourists. Several people are sitting on boxes peeling bananas and tangerines. The woman selling fruit sees me and takes a long look at the little girl in my arms.

"Vietnam?" She asks me, pointing a finger at Katherine. The woman's skin is darker and her face more weathered than the city people we have been seeing in Hanoi.

"Yes," I nod my head, "Vietnam."

Cluck! Cluck! She reaches into her basket, pulls out a tangerine, and gives it to Katherine. *Cam on*, I say. *Cam on*.

After two days in Cat Ba, the women selling fruit and trinkets along the bay have seen me walk back and forth pushing the stroller enough times that they don't ask anymore. I am still followed by the "Vietnam" echo, but now it is they who are nudging their friends, remarking to each other about her. They leave me alone, unless I come near enough for them to cluck at her. The children selling postcards are another matter. I am still swarmed wherever I go, and little ones reach in the stroller to touch her, or try to pick her up so she can play.

ON MY THIRD DAY, I hire a boat to take a private trip around the islands. 150,000 *dong*, about $9.50, for four hours, and they feed us too. It is the friend of the man who runs the Internet café next to the hotel. He leads me to a levy, and calls out to a woman in one of the bamboo-bottom skiffs. She poles her way over, and he makes arrangements for her to ferry us out to the larger motorboat.

Katherine and I sit in the middle, and I think back to a visit to a Vietnamese heritage museum in Hanoi where they had one of these boats on display as an antiquity.

We spend most of the boat trip out front on the bow. The diesel engine is old, and the inside of the boat reeks of fuel fumes. Although the day is damp and hazy, it's warm enough to not be uncomfortable. Today it's just us, weaving and winding our way around these unusual peaks. Occasionally we pass a moored 'home,' with a barking dog to warn of our presence. There is an oyster farm, marked by row after row of small white buoys. These aren't oysters for eating, my guide says. They are for pearls. The 'factory' is a floating platform, with the employees working within sight of where they pull the oysters out of the water. A girl paddles over to us, and holds out a tray. It is covered with strands of white and pink and pale gray fresh-water pearls. Single, delicate strands. Twisted, braided, looping multiple strands, shining out at me from the black cloth of the tray. They shimmer like the bellies of the oysters they were pulled from. No, I shake my head. Regretfully, I have left most of my money in the hotel safe back in Hanoi, and I will bet that I can't use a VISA floating out here on the edge of the China Sea.

When we return, Katherine and I sit along the water at one of the tables. A lone postcard girl comes over, to chat and to eat tangerines with us. She helps pick up some of the seeds that have fallen into the stroller, and wipes Katherine's mouth with a tissue. I ask to see her postcards. It has been so hazy since I've arrived that I haven't gotten any really good photo opportunities, and the area is so stunning that I don't want to go home without something to show my friends. I buy a pack...we negotiate down to 12,000 *dong*.

As I head back to the hotel, the hoard descends once again upon us. One sharp-eyed little girl sees the pack of cards that I have just bought in the pocket of the stroller.

"You said you would buy from me!" She yells. "You said yesterday 'later'!"

I did no such thing. "No I didn't," I argue back with her.

"Yes you did! You said you buy from me!" She is following me, this twelve-year old girl, yelling. I walk on, ignoring her. Finally, she yells something that I couldn't quite make out, but what it sounded like wasn't very…

"Suck my dick!" she yells again at me.

I blink, startled.

"Suck my dick!" she taunts me, her face squinching up into an ugly pucker.

"You don't have one, young lady," is the first thing that pops out of my mouth.

"Suck my dick!" she says once again.

"That is *not* a very nice thing to say. It is a nasty thing to say!" I roll my eyes and turn back towards the Sunflower. At least she has stopped following me, although I still hear her voice yelling, getting fainter as I move away. I feel a little stunned and then I realize: this is the only negative treatment that I have received from *anyone* since arriving in this country.

ON MY FOURTH MORNING, I am more than ready to climb on the bus back to where the boat will pick us up. I have walked up and down the harbor's edge a hundred times, and sat in the same chairs at the same cafes. It has been a nice change of pace but I'm ready to be back in Hanoi. Actually, I am ready to finalize the adoption. I am ready to head down to Ho Chi Minh City, where I have to submit our paperwork to U.S. Immigration. As much as I love travel, I am ready to be HOME. I am *tired*! These past few nights, easing Katherine into sleep, easing her awake, and sleeping so lightly so when she wakes in the middle of the night I can catch her before she cries out, have been successful but exhausting. Even though I'm able to gather my strength each morning, I can tell that I'm getting more and more worn down. My tolerance-level is dropping: patience with schedules and traffic…patience with Katherine at night when she won't go to sleep. Gathering our things each and every time we go out is more and more of a chore. And packing and unpacking our life each time we move on even more so.

I'm not the only one who is tired. Soon after the boat leaves for Haiphong, Katherine starts to cry. And cry. And wail. And she is inconsolable. I pick her up, put her down, leave her alone, offer her food, offer her a bottle. She screams and wails. She doesn't seem to be in pain, she just seems mad. The trip is over two hours. She screams almost the whole time. I'm feeling a little frayed. Did I say just a little? Who is this evil twin who has replaced my angelic daughter?

In Haiphong, the group stops at a restaurant to have lunch before the bus ride to Hanoi — the 2 1/2 hour bus ride. Katherine does fairly well at the restaurant. She eats almost as much as she throws on the ground. Within a half hour of loading onto the bus, however, here she goes again, only this time there isn't the noise of the boat engines to drown her out for the other passengers. I am the mother to a screaming banshee, and there's nothing I can do about it. But I can imagine what everyone else on the bus is thinking. I can't concentrate, I can't relax, I can't clear my mind, I can't even remember to breathe.

God, what am I doing? How could I presume that I can raise a child all by myself, and to work, and to deal with *this*. I can't deal with this screaming, screaming, screaming! What if she stays this way? What if the honeymoon is over, and this screeching red-faced angry baby is here to stay? The adoption isn't final yet…

I stop myself sharply. Don't even THINK that! You're exhausted! You're frayed! You haven't had any help. Everything will be fine, I tell myself hopefully…a little afraid. Everything will be OK. She cries on.

Chapter opening photograph: Ha Long Bay

九

Chapter 10

January 16th

OUTSIDE THE WINDOWS OF BINH'S SUV, it is still dark. Katherine is sleeping in my arms. Her good attitude has returned for the past couple of days, which has helped me to re-establish my mindful focus. Still, I'm pretty exhausted, but I'm so excited that I could never sleep on this trip. We are on our way to Lang Son province for the finalization of the adoption. The Giving and Receiving Ceremony.

The months of monitoring the Adoptive Parents of Vietnam list have given me a pretty good idea what to expect. Some government officials as well as the orphanage director usually attend the ceremony. Where my experience differs is that I've never read any postings from anyone who had custody of the child for a period of time beforehand. Most people have had a visit or two with their child, but it is not until this ceremony that the child is relinquished to them. That is what I expected myself until everything changed five weeks ago!

Normally for the ceremony, a caretaker accompanies the child from the orphanage. The ceremony will take place around a large table, and there are often fruit and cakes for refreshment. Everyone will make a statement, including me. I haven't thought out too much about what I will say, something brief probably. I can't imagine these serious government workers being too interested in hearing me wax poetic about the anticipated joys of motherhood.

I have also heard from the APV list that in some circumstances a relative of the child may be at the ceremony as well, if the child was not abandoned. A grandmother, perhaps. Or possibly the birthmother. Although peoples' accounts of meeting birthparents of their children at the ceremony were usually positive, I can't but wonder what I will feel if Katherine's birthmother showed up. How would she act? Would she be sad? How would she look at me? Would I feel as if I am stealing her baby away from her? Her misfortune has brought my blessing. How fair is that? What would I say to her? What would Katherine do? My arms are wrapped around Katherine's warm body. Such a big day in her life, and she is oblivious to it all.

I have brought my camera and camcorder in my backpack, but wonder how much I will get to use it. One of the curses of single-parenting is that there's never anyone around to hold the camera so both you and your child are in the same shot. I have also brought a large bag full of twenty-four children's sweater and hat sets that I bought with the Sister while we were in Hue. These are to give to the orphanage, as my mind kept going back to the shivering people that first day in Lang Son. Other than that, I haven't brought along any other gifts. The APV people sometimes mention giving little gifts, mostly symbolic, to everyone present, or having something for the orphanage workers. But right now I just don't have the presence of mind to get too complicated, so I'll just do this for the children. This visit should take a few hours, then we head straight back to Hanoi.

It is getting light as we cross the border into Lang Son province and pay the highway toll. Everything is a replay of the first trip, from the misty gray peaks, to the people and children alongside the road, to the produce and animals being transported. This time, though, when we reach the city, we drive straight to the government office building. This time, there is no child waiting for me at the orphanage. This time, my daughter is sitting with me on my lap.

We park by the side of the building and climb the stairs to the second floor. It is close to nine o'clock, and when we get to the proper offices, there are three American families there before us. Of the three children with them, two are infants, perhaps six months old, and one is a little girl of around six. They are strangers to their children, having seen them only once or twice, so they are spending some time getting to know their little ones…and the little ones are getting used to them. What discoveries they have before them! I smile. Katherine and I have been going down that road for five weeks now.

They have all used an agency that works with this orphanage, have traveled together, and their ceremonies will be together. I'll have to wait until they are finished. There are a half dozen or so Vietnamese women sitting around on the benches in the hallway, but we Americans are all waiting in the office together, getting a chance to ask each other where we are from and what the rest of our stories are. Texas. Washington State. We are all taking photos, and I ask someone for a few shots of me and Katherine sitting on the couch. Cold tea again in the teapot on the table…left over from yesterday, I guess. Perhaps the day before. There is nothing else for us to do while officials shuffle and sign papers, and carry them from room to room and back again.

I carry Katherine out into the hallway to try to relieve her boredom before fidgeting sets in. With her riding on my right hip, I point down off the balcony to the entrance hall where people are walking in and out.

"Look at all those people walking in and out!" I say to her, trying to make it sound like the most interesting thing in the world. I am slowly learning the art of making the mundane sound magnificent to keep a child occupied and entertained. With Katherine, so far this has been working, since with her history, pretty much everything is a new sight or sound or taste. The rest of the families follow us out, trying to pass the time as well. It appears that some of the Vietnamese women in the hall are the children's caretakers. They move to sit next to the children, but visibly encourage the new parents to get to know them. Perhaps among them are members of those children's birthfamilies…it is hard for me to tell. It occurs to me that one of them might be Katherine's birthmother. A mixture of anxiety and anticipation has butterflies spinning around in my gut. Those other families have someone else with whom to share this experience, a spouse, an older son or daughter traveling with them. Sharing all of the good, the bad and the volatile emotions. I have just me. Me and Katherine, that is.

Binh comes out of the room to say that the other families will have their ceremony first and that it will probably be several hours before it is our turn. "I'd like to see their ceremony, that way I'll know what to expect for mine." I tell him.

He nods, adding "Yes, we can do that."

The other families each take a seat at the fruit and candy-laden table. Each Asian child is seated on a Caucasian lap. Amazingly, there is very little squirming. None of these tiny beings are aware of the immense change that is happening in their life at this moment. None of them are aware that in a short time, they will be in a new land, with a new life and a new family.

The two officials offer a speech to the gathering in Vietnamese. Behind them is a white bust of Ho Chi Minh on a pedestal. After every few sentences they pause, and the Vietnamese agency facilitator translates into English. Outside in the hallway, the local women sit conversing with each other. They don't pay much attention to what is happening in the room even though the door is open. They have obviously been through this before. Only one woman sits to the side, wiping tears from her eyes with the heel of her hand from time to time as her friend comforts her. I can't see her face…her eyes are cast to the floor.

Katherine seems content to rest in my arms for the moment, and my thoughts stray to the woman who is responsible for bringing her into my life. I can only imagine…no…I absolutely *can't* imagine what it must have been like to give this child up, to admit to myself that I wasn't able to care for her. How crushing that must have been…how powerless and trapped she must have felt. For someone who obviously has so little in her life to call her own, to have to give away a part of herself.

One by one, the families around the table stand. One by one they give their own little speech back to the official. *We will love and care for our child. Yes, each family replies, we will teach our child about their culture and will try to someday return to Vietnam*. One by one they rise to write their names in a very large record book on the table at the front of the room.

I find myself only partially paying attention to the proceedings. Katherine's warmth, her presence, her *smell* have the attention of my senses. These have all become a part of my life over the past few weeks, will all be a part me for forever to come. Somewhere in this province not far away, Katherine's birthmother wakes up everyday. The image of her dark piercing eyes from the photograph in the documents hovers in my mind. She will never again feel the presence of the little girl who rests in my arms. As each day passes, how often will thoughts of Huong stray into her mind, wondering where she is, wondering how she is doing, wondering if she is loved? How much sadness and longing will be a part of her life? How big the lonely space in her heart?

The first ceremony has finished and it will soon be our turn. Binh is at one end of the table reading a newspaper. Katherine has sprung back to life and is reaching for some packaged cookies on the table. The wrappers crinkle enticingly, and she is more interested in unwrapping them and playing with the cellophane than she is in actually eating them. Some of the cookies I don't get away from her quickly enough, and she chucks them onto the floor.

A few more minutes and things are finally, *finally* ready to get under way. There is a new couple here. They are from Washington, D.C., and they are just turning in their paperwork. They will be meeting their child today, then flying home, only to return in six to eight weeks for the ceremony. That is the usual order of events. Leave it to me to do it my own way…but what an adventure we are having! The husband offers to tape the ceremony for me on my camcorder. What a relief. I had given up hope of having these moments recorded.

When we all take our seats, there are seven people in the room. Myself, Binh, the couple from D.C., the orphanage director, and the man and woman official. Oops, eight people. Eight including Katherine, who sits on my lap. The woman official presides. She is the same woman who tape-recorded our conversation the day I turned in my paperwork over a month ago. Behind her is a large red banner with a gold star and gold fringe along the bottom. There is a sign with Vietnamese writing, with the usual quirky English translation below in smaller letters: "Ceremony of Dilivering and Recliving Adopted." There are three bright silk flower arrangements on metal easels.

The woman official begins speaking, and Binh translates as she pauses. Mostly stuff about the government and the People of Lang Son province. The blank eyes of Uncle Ho watch from behind her back. She then gathers some papers along with the large record book for me to sign, and I move to one of the front chairs.

When I return to my seat, the woman official asks me to say a few words. Why didn't I write something down, or pay more attention when the other couples were speaking? But I haven't, so I stand up and wing it. They have been hearing this stuff all day.

"Thank you for the opportunity to adopt baby Huong." I say. Binh translates into Vietnamese, and I wait until he pauses. "I will give her a good home and good education. Thank you." I smile, nod, and take my seat while Binh wraps up my soliloquy. It feels enormously inadequate and I feel a little ashamed at not having something more important to say.

At this point, the orphanage director speaks. "We deliver baby Huong to miss Ellen for adoption," Binh translates. "We have good feeling that she agrees to adopt baby Huong. Take care of her and help her to be a good person. We wish you and baby Huong will have a good family."

The woman official speaks last, in English. "We hope you take care of baby Huong. Help her to become a good person for society. In the future, if you have good finances, if you will bring her back to Vietnam. The department requests that you report on baby Huong every year. We wish you to be happy."

THE CEREMONY ENDS, and the couple from D.C. come over to me to return my camcorder. I thank the husband profusely. What luck that they were here to do this for me. With Katherine balanced again on my hip, I turn to get the large bag full of sweaters and hats for the orphanage children that I have brought from Hue. I give it to the director, who responds to Binh, who translates back to me.

"On behalf of the children of the orphanage, I accept this gift."

Binh continues to chat with the orphanage director, and Katherine and I wait in the hallway. The other American couples have left, as have the caretakers. There is no sign of the weeping woman. I look into Katherine's eyes as she tries to wriggle her fingers between my closed lips. I'm *officially* a mommy, Katherine's mommy now. There's no going back…*forever.* I think back to Tu Niem's beautiful poem. Beautiful and wrong. This is no child who was tossed away without regard or to be trampled on the road. I have no doubt that to give Katherine, Huong, up is probably the most difficult, tortuous thing her birthmother has ever done. This is the day that our three destinies, our *duyen phan*, have come together. Soon, two of us will be carried to the other side of the world, following our path. What could I say to her if I had the chance? Thank you? I'm sorry? Your little girl will be happy? At this moment, I can't think of a thing.

Subj: Phase one down...
Date: 1/16/02 6:17:10 PM
From: Efitz
To: Vietnam Group
Sent from the Internet (Details)

Hey everyone!

Just got back tonight from Lang Son Province where our "Giving and Receiving" ceremony was performed, and now Katherine has been officially adopted by me...as far as the Vietnamese government is concerned. Have pictures and video to share when I get back. I had been hoping to do this last week, and already be in Saigon/Ho Chi Minh City by now, but we were delayed a week.

The next step is to head down to the Hanoi police station first thing in the morning to get Katherine's passport, pick it up Friday, head to Saigon Saturday, then be there when the doors open at the INS Monday morning to turn our paperwork in. Although I have preliminary approval for Katherine from the INS for a VISA (which I got before I left the States), they have to go over her paperwork before they give me the go-ahead. U.S. Immigration is very particular that everything be totally legitimate. Monday also happens to be the day that my return tickets are for (six weeks here), so that will have to be postponed as well. Hopefully they'll push my paperwork through in just a few days. EVERYONE KEEP YOUR FINGERS CROSSED!

Some families have been delayed several weeks, even months, but for irregularities that I shouldn't have trouble with. I hope.

OK, her majesty calls.

Take care, everyone, and I hope to be on a plane home at the end of next week.

Yay!

Love, Ellen

AFTER SENDING THE E-MAIL OFF, I carry Katherine outside to the cyclo stand. Phuc and the boys are kicked back as usual, chatting as they wait for business. When he sees me he jumps up and rolls his vehicle over to us.

"You go cyclo! Good! Good! You were gone for very long time! Phuc not make much money!"

"Yes, I know…" I tell him. "And I'm only here for a few days more, then we go to Ho Chi Minh City, then back to America."

"Where you go tonight?"

"Where was that place we went to…right when I first came to Hanoi?" I'm thinking back. That was over a month ago!

"We go to many many places when you first come to Hanoi," he responds.

"You know, the famous place, where all the tourists go…." Katherine and I have already assumed our position, and he has begun pedaling us down the street.

"You go to Moca Café one time…"

"No…no…that's not it…" A few blocks further and I am turning phrases over in my mind. It is short and catchy…K…K…"Kimbo!" I finally yell out.

"OH! Yes! Yes! Kimbo Café! Very famous! Yes, we go Kimbo Café!" He takes the next left, and soon we are at that crazy lit-up intersection. I carry Katherine in, pausing at the pastry case to let her take a peek. "Mmmmm! Mmmmmmmm!" she says, pointing.

After we sit down, I order some noodles with veggies, and yogurt with fruit. When our meal comes, Katherine is beside herself. She must have been exceptionally hungry, because she lays into the plate with a vengeance. There are soon noodles and sauce all over her face, all over us, and she is alternately pumping her fists up and down while shouting "yum! yum! yum! yum! yum! yum!" This is her newest routine for when she discovers something that she likes to eat. Everyone in the restaurant watches amused and transfixed. The owner of the restaurant and his wife come over. They are beaming at the good review they are getting from their littlest customer.

"What a lovely baby! What is her name?" they ask.

"Huong," I say, "Katherine Huong."

"Katherine…" they repeat, and pause. I think that they are wondering about this unusual Western name.

"Katherine is a family name…," I begin as an excuse for not being able to tell them what it means.

"Oh, we *know* Catherine!" the wife answers back, and points to the signed photograph of Catherine Deneuve on the wall behind the pastry counter. Silly me. Katherine takes this moment to let out another volley of "yum! yum! yum! yum! yum! yum!" We all smile and enjoy her enthusiasm.

"See?" I say, pointing first to the photo, then to my daughter. "Catherine likes, and Katherine likes!"

ON THE WAY BACK TO THE HOTEL, I have been wondering again about Phuc's burns. I finally call out.

"Phuc? How did you get those burns?"

"Burns are from a fire when I was a boy." he responds. "From a stove. My clothes caught on fire."

"It must have been very painful," I say.

"Yes! Yes! But it was a long time ago!"

The drama that I had envisioned evaporates from my thoughts.

"How are your children doing?" I ask him.

"They do good! Very good! They are good children!"

Katherine is beginning to nod off to sleep in my arms. If I'm lucky, we'll skip the crying fit tonight…

"Your baby is a very lucky baby!" Phuc tells me once again.

I feel her warm body through my clothes. Smell her baby smell drifting up from her hair. Crying fit or no, she is wonderful.

"She's lucky and I'm lucky too, Phuc. We're both lucky."

"Both lucky! Yes! Very, very good!"

Chapter opening photograph: Guardians at tomb, Hue, Vietnam

✝

Chapter 11

It is 92 degrees when we land in Ho Chi Minh City. It takes forever, it seems, to squeeze through the people to claim my bags and drag them off of the conveyor while trying to hold Katherine. The Asian concept of waiting in line is: "There are no lines." Since that first day in Hanoi when Binh took me to get my papers certified, I have seen that the law of the land is "every man for himself," even if you're woman. Even if you're a woman with a baby! Not that I'm looking for a red carpet and tons of special treatment, but after all of these weeks, my endurance really is being tested. This trip I have *all* of my bags with me, including the extra ones carrying my gifts and souvenirs. So it's me, Katherine, two suitcases, a sport bag, a backpack and a stroller.

Eventually, my bags are on the cart, the backpack on my back, the stroller is balanced on top of my suitcases precariously, and Katherine is balanced, well, maybe also a little precariously, in the front basket of the cart. It's one of those carts that you have to squeeze a handle on the bar as you push, or the wheels lock up, so progress is slow. When the stroller or Katherine starts to wobble, I have to let go of the handles to do some stabilizing, and our whole calliope comes to a stop.

It doesn't take long for me to find a driver, or, rather, for a driver to find me. There is a throng of them meeting the crowd calling out 'Taxi! Taxi!' When I ask one how much is it into the city to the Asian Hotel, he says seven bucks, U.S. He's got a deal.

What a difference Ho Chi Minh City is from Hanoi! No dirt roads here, or rice paddies along side of the highway. The city has grown all the way out to the airport, so our ride to the hotel is nothing but city streets and shops and hotels, and lots and lots of people. It is definitely more cosmopolitan here. I don't see the straw hats, nor women walking with their *giong ganh* that were everywhere in Hanoi. Even the signs and billboards look more 'western.'

Rough Guide has steered me to the Asian hotel, and I haggle down to $25 a night since we're staying for a few nights. I follow my usual routine and dump my bags in the room, then head downstairs with Katherine to signal to one of the ever-present cyclo drivers across the street.

"One hour," I tell him, when he rolls up to me. "Around the city, just show me around."

"Six dollars," he says, and I just smile and shake my head.

"Fifteen thousand *dong*," I reply.

He looks aghast. "Four dollars!" he demands.

I look at him intently. I'll give him the benefit of the doubt. Perhaps the going rate down South here is a little higher. *Still…*

"Thirty thousand *dong*," I say. Two bucks. That's all I'm going to pay. In my mind, I think "It's only a dollar or two here and there," but it has become the point of it. Money is such a relative thing. Here in Vietnam, I may bargain for something that would cost five times as much at home. But everything's relative to what something is worth in this country. One Starbuck's latte at home would feed a family of four for several days here.

There are two price tiers in Vietnam; one for locals, one for tourists. All the guidebooks say to expect everyone to charge you (or at least try to) double or triple the price on everything. Haggling is expected. I saw some children wearing adorable 'squeaky shoes,' shoes that have a little squeaking mechanism imbedded in the heel of the shoe so when the child steps down, each step makes a 'squeak! squeak!' I bought two pairs for Katherine, only to find out that I paid twice what they were worth later that day. My price was still only four dollars each, but I got so mad that I went back and made a scene. Even though the women at the shop surely didn't understand most of what I was saying, they got the gist of it…and handed me back twenty-thousand *dong*, laughing. I *still* paid 'tourist-tax' but I felt a little better as I walked out. And the funny thing is that I think that they got a kick out of this Western woman coming in and blowing her stack. Haggling's a game to them. I ended up being part of the entertainment.

The cyclo driver nods in agreement. Two bucks. When I climb into the seat with Katherine in my lap, I think 'that was way too easy,' and wonder if I have still gotten ripped off or not. At least I have not broken the prime rule: always set your price first.

First he takes us down along the Saigon River. Saigon is the old name for this city that was officially renamed after its 'fall' in 1975. But many people still call it Saigon. It's just easier, and habit, probably. There are huge river boats, floating restaurants, tethered along the quay waiting for the sun to set so they can begin their dinner cruises. Shamelessly large signs are posted along the sidewalk advertising each one's amenities. My driver pedals on.

He takes us past a few of the fancier hotels listed in my guidebook, the ones that I've heard mentioned on the APV list. The Rex, the Majestic, the Continental. At $70 plus a night, and with me not knowing exactly how many days we're going to be here waiting for the paperwork to get approved, I'm happy where I am.

As we turn onto Le Loi Street, I take note of the street numbers on the buildings. Today is Saturday. I have to wait until Monday to turn my paperwork in to the INS office here on Le Loi, which is about five blocks from my hotel. I *will* be here bright and early. I've got my preliminary approval document from the Norfolk INS office, but they now have to check out all of my Vietnamese paperwork to make sure that it is in order. Their main concern is that children are not obtained through monetary compensation of, or improper inducement to, any parent or parents.

A few more turns and we pass Notre Dame cathedral. Thank goodness we are a moving target, as I can see the postcard and trinket sellers descending upon those on foot. The European-looking cathedral looks less out of place here in Ho Chi Minh City than the cathedral did in old town Hanoi. Everywhere I look there are Westerners, and the sight of me with Katherine creates no curious stares like it did in Hanoi. I have little doubt that Saigon residents have seen a lot more of the outside world and foreigners than their counterparts up north. The whole city has a faster pace, and the whole look and feel is decidedly more cosmopolitan, from the clothes that people are wearing to the orderliness. It is crowded, but the blocks are in a planned grid. There are *real* traffic lights at most intersections, and cars and motorbikes *really* stop at them. After Hanoi, it seems a lot more like home, but not necessarily in all the good ways. It doesn't have the charm that I have come to appreciate in Hanoi. I'm sure it has its own charm in its own way, but, after one and a half months of traveling, I don't plan on sticking around long enough to find out. Nothing personal, but I am ready to head home, recover, relax and begin a new life with my daughter.

My daughter. Katherine is taking this new place in with her usual unruffled demeanor. Just another cyclo ride to her, lots of lights, sounds and people. She watches everything, but nothing startles or surprises her. She rests back in my arms like she has done it forever. Perhaps she has…in other lifetimes.

FOR A DAY AND A HALF, we wander around. I get to do my final shopping, mostly for stuff that's breakable, like lacquer-ware. Up until now, I didn't want to worry about carting around any fragile stuff. We chat and mingle with people in shops and on the street. I had tried so hard up in Hanoi to pronounce my few Vietnamese words correctly, and now I am being giggled at. The southern accent is different. Up in Hanoi, 'thank you', *cam on*, is pronounced as two distinct chopped syllables: '*gam on*.' Here in Saigon, they blend the words together, and it sounds more like 'gammon' as in the game, backgammon. My coffee that I have been enjoying so much, café *sua*, sounds like 'soo-AH,' two abrupt syllables up north, but here it sounds more like you're saying 'sweet' without the 'eet.' 'Café Swa.' I get the impression that they are charmed that I am trying.

The Continental Hotel is a short block walk from the Asian, and its elegant façade seems to whisper past secrets and the presence of colonial high society. Writers from Somerset Maugham to Graham Greene tossed back drinks and spun tales on the now-gone terrace. It sits overlooking the Municipal Theatre and Lam Son Square, which, if you see the movie remake of Greene's *The Quiet American*, you'll get to see it explode into flames and violence.

We turn down Le Loi and walk down the park-like median towards a multi-tiered fountain. Children come up to us offering cold coconut water from coolers. Straws protrude out from the hairy brown husks. As we cross to the sidewalk, a teenage girl leading her blind grandmother asks us for money. A shop sells painted wooden wall decorations adorned with Disney characters from Mickey Mouse to Dalmatians. A gallery nearby sells reproductions of famous European paintings, and a young man sits out front with his easel, working on a Dutch landscape. A bent-over, gray-haired woman slowly makes her way over the pavement. In her right hand is a knotted rope that pulls a piece of plywood mounted on wheels. On the board is a withered man lying on his back, looking up at the awnings and the sky. His pant legs are empty and folded over just below his pelvis. The woman's gnarled left hand is held out, stretching towards each person that she passes.

BACK IN THE ROOM, we rest and get away from the heat. I go over our upcoming itinerary, what we have left to do, in my head. I've already postponed my flight. The tickets home are dated for Sunday the 20th, which is tomorrow. I e-mailed my travel agent before I left Hanoi to stand by for the new return date. The first thing we have to do is to turn in our paperwork to the INS and have an interview. The paperwork is already in a file folder in my backpack ready to go. Then we have to go to Cho Ray hospital for Katherine's U.S. visa physical exam. That's a taxi ride across town. The INS processes my paperwork, then forwards it to the U.S. Consulate if everything is in order. When we are notified, we go to the Consulate for our visa interview and to pay for Katherine's visa. Once her visa is ready, we can go home. Theoretically, this can take just a few days. If, however, they are backed up with many families, or if the INS wants to check any of my information, there can be delays. Of days — of weeks. I remember reading on the APV before I left there have been families lately who had questionable items on their paperwork according to the INS. Families that are still here right now. It comes down to whether or not the children are legally considered orphans by the United States. Vietnam's criteria for an orphan are less stringent that the U.S.'s, and it is possible for a U.S. citizen to adopt a child in Vietnam, and be considered the parent there, only to not be allowed to bring the child into the U.S. because the INS says the child was not an orphan. It is the nightmare that all of us dread, an unlikely but haunting possibility. Yes, if Katherine's paperwork is in order, there shouldn't be a question. But wouldn't those other families have had their paperwork in order, too? And here I am, doing an independent adoption without an agency who has done this dozens, or hundreds, of times checking up on me. I just have to trust that in all of the lists I compiled, in all of the checking and rechecking, I didn't leave something out.

Just a block down the street is an upscale shopping mall with some professional office space attached. It turns out that Korean Air's Ho Chi Minh City office is right here, and I go in to check what I will have to do to re-schedule my flight. The woman at the desk is very friendly, and she smiles and clucks at Katherine.

Her name is Katherine," I tell her, "Katherine Huong."

"Huong!" she replies, her smile getting even bigger. "It means perfume." She is so soft-spoken that I almost have to ask her to repeat herself.

"Yes, I've been told."

"My name is Hang. It means moon."

Katherine and I pass a few minutes criss-crossing the carpeted floor of the office, me holding her hands as she practices her toddling, while Hang checks my previous itinerary and figures out what I'll have to do to rebook. On the walls are Korean Air posters. 'Morning Calm' is printed on tranquil scenes of sunrises, snow-capped mountains and misty rivers. Apparently 'Morning Calm' is both Korea's official motto and the airline's as well. The Land of Morning Calm.

I tell her that I hope to be heading back this weekend. Unfortunately, with my original travel agent being in Vancouver, the half-a-world-away time difference makes it the middle of the night there. She says that the way the ticket is issued, it might only be possible for them to rebook it on the originating end. She sends an inter-office communication to the U.S. branch of Korean Air, and says that she should hear something back tomorrow.

Hang also warns me that this weekend flights are either booked or require additional transfers through Bangkok or Hong Kong, with layovers. Whatever it takes, I'm going to be flying across the Pacific on *something* this weekend. There is also the matter of changing the ticket for my daughter, from Le Thi Thanh to La Thi

Huong. Whenever something like this comes up, it reminds me of the little girl back in Lang Son. How differently things happen from what we expect sometimes. I don't worry for that little girl. She will be shortly adopted, there is no doubt in my mind, after seeing the number of families coming and going in the Lang Son province offices. She will probably be on her way to Europe very soon. There are more adoptions from Vietnam to the European countries than to the U.S., and from what I've heard from the other families, their requirements aren't as strict.

"Thank you, Hang. I will come back tomorrow."

MONDAY MORNING, JANUARY 21st, 8:30 AM. The INS office. 65 Le Loi Street, 9th floor, Saigon Center. Sign on the door: In observance of the Martin Luther King, Jr. holiday, this office will be closed on Monday January 21st. We will reopen on Tuesday, January 22nd. Damn!!! I've been out of the country so long that I'm totally out of the loop. In all of Ho Chi Minh City, there are two offices closed today. The INS and the U.S. Consulate.

Katherine and I ride the elevator back down to the lobby. The hospital's not closed, I suddenly realize. Back down Le Loi we go, to Dong Khoi, hang a left at the Continental Hotel, and one block to the Asian to get the address and directions of the hospital that I have written down. On the taxi ride over, I hope that there aren't any special forms that I need from the INS first. I'm putting my faith in my luck. It's served me well so far; well, except for the INS office being closed this morning!

At the hospital, the woman at the information desk is not sure where to send me. She makes a few phone calls, then asks an assistant to lead Katherine and I upstairs to a doctor who speaks better English than she does. The doctor sends us back downstairs, and around to the back of the hospital. We go to a completely different building. Everywhere there are people sitting around on benches waiting. They are in the main building, in this annex, even outside on benches under the shade of the trees. They look pretty hunkered down, like they know that this is going to be one long wait. At the entrance to the annex, there is a sign that says "visa examinations." At least *that* is straightforward. There is a sign-in table in the front hall, and the woman sitting there passes me a clipboard with a form on it that I fill out for Katherine.

"Do you have her photos?" she asks when I pass the clipboard back to her.

"Photos?" I question back. "I didn't know that I needed any photos…" She shows me some of the other forms on the table. Apparently, to have an appointment for any reason at the hospital, you need to bring in your own passport-sized photos, which are attached to your entry form.

"I don't have any, but I'm sure that there's a place not far."

She stops to ponder this glitch in procedure. I hate the thought of having to go back out to the street looking for a photo shop. Sure, they tend to be everywhere, but in the meanwhile, more people are going to get in ahead of us here.

Finally she nods. "You can go in and get started. Your appointment with the doctor won't be until after lunch, so you can bring the pictures then." She points down the hall behind her, and tells me to go to the room on the left. Her English, like many Vietnamese here in Ho Chi Minh City, tends to be better than most people's up north. Not surprising, with their close ties to us Americans once upon a time.

We walk down the hall and into a room where we wait just a few minutes before Katherine's name is called. I use the time to finish filling out the form on the clipboard. Katherine shrieks and cries as they measure her body and head, and weigh her. Not exactly painful stuff, but she is definitely a 'don't mess around with me' baby. At fourteen months, she is still seven kilos, about fifteen pounds. I'm not too up on comparisons, as I've never been one to sit with moms back home and chit chat about pounds and months, but I'm pretty sure that she's setting up to be *une petite jeune fille*. A little young lady. Katherine will be lucky to make it much over five feet. Petite. Petite and perfect.

Our appointment is set for two o'clock, so we head out to find lunch and a photo shop, not necessarily in that order. This end of town is a little more commercial, definitely not touristy. Occasionally we are forced out into the street by lack of a sidewalk, or it being simply impassable. Because of it not being a tourist region, it is several blocks before I see a photo shop. They want six bucks for two little passport photos. I don't think so! I know that it's only a few bucks, but the going rate back near the hotel is about two. I can't bring myself to do it, so we head on down the road. Surely there's another one not much farther down. There always is. Four more blocks, and no photo shop, but I do see on a corner a hole-in-the-wall noodle shop, filled with locals. As I stop to look at my map, Katherine is making friends with the grandmother working the soup cauldron. The shop seems to be a family affair, with three generations cooking, serving, clearing and making way for the new customers that flow in. Must be a good place. The table-traffic is heavy.

"She is hungry," grandmother says, indicating Katherine. Actually, she doesn't *say* that. She speaks to me in Vietnamese, but by now it's pretty obvious to me what she means.

Katherine adores noodles, whether she is hungry or not, so I'm not going to argue. We take a seat, and while I order the special (um, that would be: noodle soup), the daughter makes sure that Katherine's noodles are cut up and that she has some soft veggies in it too. None of them speak English, but it really doesn't matter. Everything's right out here overflowing through the front of the shop and out onto the sidewalk, so all you have to do is point. And it's open air, so as we sit and relax we watch the traffic roll, walk, pedal and whiz by. The honking of horns isn't as bad here as it is in Hanoi.

With lunch wrapped up, at 12,000 *dong*, I have an hour to get those photos and make it back to our appointment. The thought crosses my mind that I might have to go back to that first shop and just shell out the six bucks. I refuse give in that easily. We set out in a new direction, and two blocks later, on the other side of the street, I see a Fuji sign. Victory! Only I wonder what they're going to charge me. Even if it's six bucks again, I don't have much choice.

The shop is another family business, and there is a toddler a little older than Katherine waddling around in his pair of squeaky shoes. Katherine watches the little boy intently. I ask the man behind the counter how much for the two photos. 45,000 *dong*, he says. Three bucks. He leads us upstairs to where he has a white backdrop set up as reflective lighting. Ten minutes later we are making our way back to the hospital. Grandmother waves to us as we round her corner.

I have been told that this hospital is the only place in Ho Chi Minh City that is authorized to do the U.S. visa physicals. When we get to the appointment, the exam consists of listening to her breathing and heartbeat, looking in her mouth and ears, and asking me if she has shown any signs of sickness. Nope, just me. I've been nursing a sore throat for four days now, and eating lozenges like candy. But she's been fine. Her form is marked approved, and placed in a sealed envelope with a stamp to prevent tampering. Hopefully it will not be too many days before I'm delivering this to the U.S. Consulate.

TUESDAY, JANUARY 22ND. 9 A.M. At least I saw the posted hours when I was here yesterday, so I had a more leisurely breakfast this morning. I am the first one into the waiting room at the INS office. The staff aren't even behind their glass-fronted windows yet. I take a seat in the front row with Katherine pulled up beside me in her stroller. I glance over at a bulletin board and idly read some of the posted notices to American citizens. Safety warnings and procedures implemented since 9/11. Consulate policies. Office memoranda. A woman slides into a seat behind the window furthest to the right. No one else is here, and I take my packet of papers up to her. She has one more form for me to fill out, my I-600 form. In Norfolk, I had gotten my I-600A form, which is the one you use for adoption but when the child hadn't been identified yet. Now that Katherine is here in flesh and blood, I get to file this permanent form.

As I finish the form, the waiting room door opens, and I see several familiar faces. It is the three families that I met in Lang Son, with little ones in tow. No matter where you adopt from in Vietnam, everybody ends up right here in this room in Ho Chi Minh City, and then the U.S. Consulate. We are compatriots in this adventure, and will get to know each other even better now: we will share the wait for our interviews this morning.

My challenge now is to keep a lively fourteen-month old entertained in a room filled with only chairs and people. For several hours. The infants are too young to be of much interest to Katherine, and the six-year old has a temper tantrum and is removed down the hall and into the elevator by her new father. So we have crawling races, and I push my back to the limit supporting her in her toddling efforts. We empty, sort and re-sort the contents of the diaper bag. This is especially intriguing to Katherine, as mommy keeps this bag off-limits most of the time. Mommy, however, is fatigued and getting desperate. Thankfully, this last resort keeps her somewhat occupied until our name is called at eleven-fifteen. I gather up our things and we are escorted to a bright office for the interview. Through the windows, I see the city of Saigon spreading out around us.

Our interviewer, on loan from the Bangkok office due to the workload here in Ho Chi Minh City, runs through a list of questions, most of which double-check against the information in our paperwork. Where does Katherine come from, and what do I know about her history? Why isn't the name of my agency filled in? I explain that being the gung-ho kinda gal that I am, I did it myself. When he wonders why, I tell him that I save about ten thousand dollars this way. He's silent, but nods…apparently it's acceptable, but highly unusual. On my lap, my hands clasp my own stack of papers. I had on one of my lists that they would ask for financial data, old 1040's, bank statements, so that I could justify that I could support this child. He never gets around to asking for this data that I have painstakingly made copies of. I guess he figures that if you can afford to go through this adoption process in the first place, then you can afford to support the child.

And that is it. I guess because of the high-profile trouble that some families have been having, I was prepared for the third degree. I was prepared to go through document after document. But that *really* is it, as the interviewing officer jots down a few notes, and cross-checks some things with some of the pages in the stack that is my dossier.

"Thank you," he tells me.

Thank you, back.

TWENTY-FOUR HOURS LATER, we are spending most of our time in the hotel room, waiting for our call. They don't tell you when it will come, so you hope for the best, and that you won't be a prisoner for too long. At least it's cool in here. Again it's over ninety degrees outside. I am trying to keep Katherine entertained right now with MTV. We conduct to the music together. It's a heavy metal program at the moment. She's got a two-hand action swing-thing going, and the livelier the music gets, the more she likes it. I'm experiencing 'proud parent aptitude syndrome,' which happens anytime your child picks up and does something you consider particularly brilliant. It obviously will determine future career direction. Right now I'm thinking that she will be an outstanding musician, and am deciding which instrument I will start her out on. Piano, for sure, as it's a cornerstone. But after that…

At four o'clock the phone rings. It is a woman from the INS. I half expect her to tell me that I have to come in to answer some more questions. There are a few things the examiner overlooked. But no, she just gives me a short message: my file has been forwarded to the Consulate. I can go over in the morning to apply for Katherine's visa. That's it.

And this *is* it. This is *really* it. Nothing left now but to get her visa and go home. No more questions, no more potential surprises. No more worry that after all of this someone won't say "Wait a minute! You forget something!" and that something happens to be a little piece of paper sitting at home on my dining room table, and Katherine can't leave the country without it. We, mother and daughter, are really going to get to go home.

The Lang Son contingent are all present and accounted for early in the morning when the consulate opens up. They received their call yesterday afternoon as well. American citizens get special priority at the entrance, and we whip past the Vietnamese waiting in line. The U.S. Consulate on Le Duan Street is built on the site of the old U.S. Embassy, the one from the movies where helicopters lifted people off of the roof during the fall of Saigon in 1975. Now the scene is cool and calm, with ceiling fans turning high overhead, and rows of benches in the waiting area where you sit to wait for your number to be called. 'American-style' waiting in line. What a difference from Hanoi. And their airports.

The wait is much shorter today, as this is more just a visit to turn in the final proper forms, and to submit four passport-sized photos of Katherine, taken ¾ view from the right. We are finished within the hour, and upon leaving, the woman we have met with says that we can return at four o'clock to pick up her visa.

"Today?" I ask.

Yes, I heard right. Today. After we pick up this one last thing we are completely done, finished.

"Hang!" I call excitedly, walking through the doors of the Korean Air office. "Can you get me home tonight? We're done!" Hang has such a quiet demeanor, and this office is so new and crisp and calm, but I can't help myself but bring in a little American noise and excitement.

"You are finished?" she asks me. "That was very fast!"

"Yes, and I'm ready to go home!"

"I will see what I can do." and she hops onto her computer. I had stopped back by the other day, but she said that she would have to wait until I knew my departure date to see how my tickets would have to be issued.

"I can get you on the direct flight to Seoul tonight. There are seats. And since the rest of your flight uses exactly the same legs that your cancelled tickets are for, I can issue it all right now. Seoul to Dallas, Dallas to Norfolk."

I can hardly believe it. Even at my most optimistic, I wouldn't have guessed that I would be on a flight home instead of going to sleep in Ho Chi Minh City tonight. Christ, I'm not packed, I need to e-mail home to make sure that I get picked up at the airport in Norfolk. Then I need to settle up at the hotel…

I flinch a little when I see the itinerary. My flight is at 1:00 a.m., which means check-in at the airport at 11:00 p.m.. On the one hand, that gives me plenty of time to get things done. On the other hand, I hope that Katherine sleeps through the whole thing in her stroller.

Subj: Gooooooood Morning (from) Vietnam!
Date: 1/24/02 12:58:17 PM
From: Efitz
To: Vietnam Group
Sent from the Internet (Details)

YAY! Paperwork's DONE everyone! And boy am I ready to get home! ETA: Norfolk Airport, Saturday 2:25 p.m. via Dallas.

The moment that she sets foot in Dallas, Katherine will automatically become a U.S. citizen. Wow!

(Katherine's about 45 minutes into her usual one-hour nap, so we'll see how long this gets! Fortunately, the stroller drops back so she can sleep while I type.)

Did I tempt fate or what? Guess who just sat up and said pay attention to me?? OK, more later, maybe, but wanted to share the good news!

By the way, thanks everyone for all the well-wishes along the way, even if I wasn't able to respond to them all due to less-than-optimal Internet connections. They were/are much appreciated!

Love, Ellen

AFTER ALMOST TWO MONTHS AWAY FROM HOME, it is sort of unreal that I'll soon be back home in Norfolk again. My brother, who will be picking me up at the airport and who has stayed in my house to take care of it and the dog and cat these past two months, says that it snowed ten inches in one day last week. In Norfolk! And I missed it. Considering that hardly anyone in Norfolk owns a snow shovel, including me, maybe that's not such a bad thing.

In some ways this trip has flown by so fast, and in others it has lingered slowly to allow me to savor it. The worst part right now is that I definitely have something unsavory attacking my tonsils. As wonderful as Katherine's behavior has been, exceptional in fact, the on again, off again lack of sleep that comes with babies has really worn me down. My throat has gotten worse this past week, but I've had no other option than to refuse to get sick. It's just me and her. I'll have to make one more trip to the pharmacy across the street from the hotel for a final supply of lozenges for the flight.

In spite of the panicy, excited craziness that I feel, I manage to have time for a stroll around downtown one last time in the afternoon. Everything is, amazingly, scrunched into my bags. Katherine slept earlier on the way home from the Consulate and during my final Internet session, so I have no hope of a nap with her in the room. I could really use a babysitting nun right now, because I know that it's going to be a long night.

THURSDAY, JANUARY 24TH, 11:00 P.M., Tan Son Nhat Airport, Ho Chi Minh City. After being dropped off at the curb by the taxi, I struggle with the cart, bags, stroller, child, and that confounded dead-man's-grip handle on the cart. Things wobble, I weave, and the crowd is oblivious as I try to push my way through. Eleven at night must be rush hour here. Either that, or it's always rush hour here. What I would give right now for someone to say "can I help you with that?" I think that I would collapse from the shock of it. But it doesn't happen. So I don't.

There are no tranquil posters of pristine scenes here. It ain't morning, and it ain't calm. It's the middle of the night and it is chaos. After waiting in line, what there might even be of one, for twenty minutes, Katherine decides that this isn't interesting or fun anymore. She starts to cry. Wail, really. And believe it or not, it has a positive effect: I get pushed to the front and up to the desk. Where no one would help or even make way for a struggling woman with my bags, an unhappy baby is another matter. The child *must* be appeased!

Her timing is perfect. You can stop now, Katherine. Only she doesn't stop. It is past midnight. She cries through the second bag check. She cries as we go down the long hallway to the waiting area. She cries in spite of the fluffy stuffed pig that I buy with the last *dong* that I have on me. She cries and cries and cries. People stop me from time to time, telling me what I should do to get her to stop crying. I'm sick. I'm exhausted. She doesn't want food, she doesn't want to be held, she doesn't want to be patted, jiggled or rubbed. She's tired, and if she would just fall asleep. *Just leave me the hell alone and don't tell me what I need to do to get her to stop crying and don't look at me like that, I'm not torturing her and I'm not a horrible mother!*

IF IT HAD NEVER OCCURRED TO ME before in my pre-mommy life, I know so very well now. Whatever mental state one may be in, no matter how educated or composed the person may be, a crying child will deteriorate that mental state until you are an agitated mass of brainless jellyfish. I can't even find an empty corner alone so I can sit and roll her back and forth. There are people in every square inch of the joint. I finally secure a spot in a seat behind one of the large-screen TV's. At least the two noises sort of run together...they can compete to drown each other out.

At the gate, they take my stroller, and I carry Katherine against my right shoulder the rest of the way. She is only half-heartedly squirming and whining now, fading into the familiar "yi-yi-yi" that I know precedes sleep. They have given me a bulkhead seat, and after take-off, they fasten a little bed to the wall in front of me for Katherine, which she tolerates not one little bit. Here we go again. She is beyond tired, and this little bit of fussing has gotten her fired up again. All of my intellectual prowess can do nothing in the face of this, my daughter's, fit of rage and exhaustion. An hour later we are on the floor, outside of one of the service bays. Katherine lies face down on a blanket and finally falls asleep to the deep rumbling and vibration of the engines. I'm propped against the wall, half dazed, half watching to make sure that nobody steps on her. She gives me a few hours, not to sleep, but at least try to gather what is left of my nerves.

IT IS DAWN WHEN WE ARRIVE IN SEOUL, KOREA: the Land of Morning Calm. Fortunately for Katherine (and more so for me!), it is that. She got maybe four hours of sleep, and I snatched perhaps two, if I add the bits and pieces together. It has been over twenty-four hours since I woke up yesterday. The airport is brand new, spotlessly clean and full of early sunlight streaming in the new, spotlessly clean, and full of early sunlight streaming in the windows. Katherine seems to be refreshed, somehow, after the night on the plane, and is her usual bright and chipper self.

We have a six-hour layover here, and I happen upon a separate room that is a children's play area. What a great idea for an airport! Although I can't get any sleep, at least there's a closed door so I can relax my usual vigilance. Katherine is distracted by three American military kids, and a brother and sister from India. She is the littlest of the bunch, so they make her the focus of their play. It is here that Katherine scoots her feet under her, rises up, and takes two wobbly steps forward before she falls down. Did I just see what I thought I saw? Katherine's first solo steps, here in the Seoul Airport. An auspicious beginning for a world traveler. Although that's all that she attempts, she is quite pleased with herself and with the fuss that I make over it. Don't forget to write it in the journal…as if I'd forget that.

LEG TWO. SEOUL TO DALLAS. Pass on the bulkhead. We're in the last row of the middle section. There is no one between me and Katherine on one aisle, and an American teenager on the other aisle. That leaves five empty seats between us for the longest leg of the trip. Surely we'll get some sleep now! We can all just about stretch out. I can hardly wait.

Over thirteen hours in the air later, Katherine has slept for about five of it. I have slept maybe two, in fifteen and twenty minute intervals. Twice she rolled off of the seats and onto the floor. The other nine hours, she was awake. Totally. And wanting to be entertained. That will go on the list as one of the hardest things I have ever done in my life, counting college and board exams and, oh, just about everything else. Keeping this child happy and not crying while I could feel my last reserves of energy being hacked away little by little.

Thank God my teenaged friend at the other end of the row had babysitting experience. She, thankfully, took over when Katherine crawled over in her direction. Which was pretty much when mommy stopped being physically able to walk her up and down aisles and hoist her around. I'm so tired I can't even fall asleep now, and all I can do is watch the video screen at the front of the rows that shows where the plane is relative to the Pacific Ocean, over the Aleutians, on to mainland North America, the Rockies, then to Texas. That little plane moves so slowly. So slowly.

WHEN WE LAND IN DALLAS, it is Saturday morning. I have been basically awake since Thursday morning, Vietnam time, which would make it...Wednesday night American time. Going on three days.

Dallas. Katherine has touched down on American soil. The stewardess makes an announcement about U.S. Customs. Heavy sigh. I forgot about that. I had blindly said goodbye to my luggage not expecting to see it again until Norfolk. Customs means that I have to pick everything back up, carry it all through customs and then recheck it again. I make my way down to baggage claim with Katherine in her usual post on my right hip. My whole right arm and shoulder are starting to ache from carrying her, but it's still stronger than my left. I claim a baggage cart, and wait while I watch suitcases, boxes, and duffle bags, most with duct tape around them, come spouting out from down below to start their journey round and round on the conveyor belt. I half laugh when I realize that there is another Beatles song that has been going through my head for the past several hours, like a soundtrack turned way down low: "I'm soooo tired, I haven't slept a wink, I'm soooo tired, my mind is on the blink..." Thank God she's not crying, thank God she's not crying, thank God she's not...this has become my mantra. Katherine, amazingly, is awake and reasonably cheerful in spite of her own lack of sleep. I have no idea what time of day she thinks it is.

As I start to struggle with one of the bags, keeping one eye on Katherine to make sure that she doesn't try to make a break for it, I hear: "Can I help you with that, ma'am?" There is a blue-jeaned, cowboy-hatted older gentleman offering to help me lift my bag. GOD BLESS AMERICA!! I know that I'm home now! Other than the tourists in Hue and Ha Long Bay, no unpaid stranger has offered to lift anything for me for almost two months. Yes, please. Thank you very, very much. And could you also get that one there, too? God bless America, I repeat to myself.

Just on the other side of customs is our next stop. The immigration office. We have a sealed envelope from the INS in Ho Chi Minh City, and this is where it gets delivered. There are only a few people here, and we wait for twenty minutes while through the windowed wall I watch the hordes of people from flight after flight pile through customs and head off to their connecting flights. I now hold an American citizen in my arms.

It isn't until I recheck my luggage that I realize that I forgot the stroller back on the conveyor belt before the customs line. That was half an hour and a tram ride ago, and there is no way that I'm going back for it.

Weighed down with just my little girl, the backpack and the diaper bag, I find a spot on the carpet near our gate. Katherine is munching on a chicken taco from Taco Bell. Shredded lettuce and yellow cheese scatter on the floor around her feet. A woman in the seats near us had initiated a game of peek-a-boo with Katherine. She has 'I'm a grandmother' written all over her. We get into a conversation about Katherine, and she is charmed by the story.

She begins pointing to me, asking Katherine "Is this your mama? Is this your mama?"

Katherine watches her intently, but does nothing.

"Mama. Mama," my new friend says, pointing. "Ma MA!" drawing it out, pausing between syllables.

"MaMa." Katherine says quietly.

I blink. That is the first time that she has said mama, and this woman has pulled it out of her in less than five minutes.

"Good! Yes, that's right, Ma ma!"

"Ma ma." Katherine says again, a little more loudly, a little more sure of herself.

Yes, my daughter. That's right. Mama. As tired as I am, I smile.

THEY FINALLY BEGIN BOARDING for this last leg of my trip. I am almost home. This is the first time in my life that I have been able to jump up when they announce "passengers with small children may board now." I can barely hold Katherine, my arms are so weak and shaking. They take my ticket and run it through the counter. A long, high-pitched beep goes off. The security guard comes over and says that the machine randomly picks passengers for a carry-on search. I'm 'it' today. I'm incredulous, I cannot believe this, but I don't even have the energy to do anything other than follow him over to the tables by the window and watch him while he goes through all of my bags. I stand woodenly while I hold Katherine, lacing my fingers together so my weak arms won't drop her while he runs a scanner over the both of us. I just want to be home. Please, nothing else until I'm home. Passengers are filing in in front of me, and now I have to wait in the long line on the ramp while everyone stashes their luggage and takes their seats. So much for the 'passenger with a small child' getting a break.

Buckled in and ready for takeoff, I'm on the aisle of the first coach row. There are two flight attendants sitting facing me in their own seats. Katherine has refused a bottle, has refused to snack on the little bag of chips that I have brought. She has had enough once again, and now is the time for yet another emotional blowout. As we lift off, she starts to shriek, with huge crocodile tears streaming down her cheeks, red-faced and getting louder. She throws the bottle down. She throws her stuffed bear down. All she wants is to sit there on my lap and cry. All I can do is to sit there in a daze and cry with her.

"It's because of the pressure," one of the flight attendants says, trying to be helpful, "it hurts her ears."

Lady, you have no idea. No idea.

Chapter opening photograph: Monks of Tu Hieu, chanting

Chapter 12

January 29th

HOME. Katherine and I have been back home for two days now. Except that this isn't Katherine, the little angel-child that I adventured with for two months in Vietnam. Somewhere between Southeast Asia and Norfolk, Virginia, the evil twin has once again taken the place of my lovely daughter. She is hysterical every moment that she is not physically attached to me. When I do hold her, she burrows into me, like she's trying to climb inside of me, trying to pull what energy she can out of my body. But I don't have any to give. I have no chi left, my little chi-sucker. I can't even put a video in and sit her on the couch next to me. She screams and glares at me with angry eyes. I can read those eyes, too: what evil twin has taken the place of my mommy? Where did that nice lady go?

That nice lady is sicker than she has been in twenty years. I have a fever, a scarlet throat and am coming down with a raging sinus infection. I am so exhausted from the last week of my trip and the flight home, that I have no juice left for her. And the more she screams, the more that I glare back at her. I know what she needs. She needs all of me, she needs all of me all of the time, but there isn't hardly anything left of me to give her. And I'm not getting the chance to get well, let alone recharge. Taking a shower is an ordeal of putting her in a playpen while she screams and stares down the hallway, holding onto the top edge, stamping her feet, while the video I put on plays unwatched behind her. After fifteen minutes with no let up, I am dressed and half-consciously go into the living room and pick her up. As soon as I do, she stops crying and turns and watches the video. Arghhh! It is all I can do to not start yelling *stop it! Stop it! Stop it! STOP CRYING! JUST STOP CRYING!*

Help me, I cry to myself, sitting on the couch at night after she finally has cried herself to sleep. I can't do this. How am I going to do this? What have I done? I can't even call and ask family to come down to help, because at the moment, they are all up in New Jersey at the side of a family member dying of cancer. They need to be there.

I feel wicked and terrible for not having extreme patience and understanding with her. I have no Buddhist practice left. I can't remember how to breathe. I know that she wants our old routine back, where she is with me 24/7 and rarely out of my sight. She can't have it, and I'm the bad guy. I have to get well enough to work. I have to find daycare.

DAYCARE! I have spent three days on the phone calling every listing in the yellow pages while Katherine sits crying in her highchair. There is not a single spot anywhere for this one little child. The waiting lists are six months minimum. *Why the hell is it so hard to find daycare?* What do people do when they have babies, call and reserve their spot as soon as the little pink plus sign shows up on the test strip? This is ridiculous! If I could only find somewhere for Katherine, then I could get some rest. If I could rest, I could get well. If I could get well, we just might have a fighting chance of getting through this. As it is, though, we seem to sink lower with each day that passes. The more she wants to cling and suck the chi out of me, the less I can stand to be with her. I have no chi left to give you, sweetheart. I don't even have any left for me.

THE DAYS SEEM TO DRAG ON FOREVER. They are filled with trying to keep her happy on my lap, or listening to her crying if she can't be, and trying to cook, clean and do laundry. And nap, maybe, if she naps. If. Then there is the poop. Between picking up after the dog outside, cleaning the cat box inside and changing diapers, it seems as if my whole life is poop. How apropos.

Our sixth day back…has it really only been six days? I get an affirmative answer from a childcare facility located in a Christian church half an hour's drive away. Yes, they can take her. When? Can you take her today? Like in one hour? The woman laughed. Yes, they can. *Halleluiah*! We are in the car before you can say "Jesus Saves" five times fast.

When we get to the church, everyone is very nice. They are quite curious about Katherine. They have never had a child with a story like hers before. I get a grand tour of the place, fill out the paperwork, and make sure they have her diaper bag. "Is she walking yet?" they ask me. Well, I respond, it's a funny thing. She took some steps on the way home in the Korean Airport, but since we've been back, she's been refusing to walk, cruise the furniture, or even just stand on her own. It's like she has purposely regressed herself to try to make me pick her up more. All she'll do is sit there. Sit there and cry. "She'll be fine," they say. "Go home and get some rest."

As I leave the room, I see Katherine's face collapse. Her cries are cut short by the closing door. God, I feel so wretched! Sorry, honey, mommy has to go and find her sanity. She doesn't know where she left it, but I'm sure that it's around here somewhere.

Walking down the steps to the parking lot, I feel lighter. I feel relief. I take in a deep breath of air. Oh yeah…*breathing*! It's salty. The church happens to be located three blocks from the wide mouth of the Chesapeake Bay. I realize that I haven't taken a deep, long breath in...in...I can't remember when I last paid attention to my breath. Weeks. Thank God it's automatic, because I'd have long been dead from forgetting to breathe. It always seems as if the good habits in life, eating right, exercising, and remembering to breathe, are the first things to go when things get heavy. Which is exactly when you need them the most. It seems hard to hold on to a thought, they come and go out of my mind these days without leaving so much as footprints behind. Right now, all I can ruminate on is the fact that I've lost my practice, and I don't know if I have the energy to get it back. Just the idea of exerting energy for anything is overwhelming. Maybe after a nap...

DRIVING HOME, I am so fully aware of the silence that envelops me in the car. Silence. In half an hour, I will be climbing into my bed, and hopefully will have a chance to start recovering from, not just jet lag, from everything. We had such an adventure, such fun, but it is not until now that I finally realize what a toll it took on me physically and mentally. Emotionally as well. What a test for my fortitude. I take another deep breath. Well, I hope that I passed the test. Actually, I know that I did. We're here, we're safe and we just need to get through this.

IT'S SUNDAY, and we've been back for two weeks. On Tuesday, her third day in daycare, they called and told me to pick Katherine up...she had a fever. So it has been just the two of us again all this week. It has been a long, *long* week. This morning I dropped Katherine off at a friend's house, and came back home to collapse on the couch. I have a screaming headache and can barely open my eyes for the light. I've had a fever of 102 for two days. My whole face feels like a toothache. Last night Katherine was crying in her crib, and when I went in to check on her, she had pulled her socks off and her feet were freezing. I lay down on my bed with her, warming them against my feverish neck. The phone rings. It's Allen.

"Hey, how are you doing?"

I burst into tears.

"What's the matter?" he asks, sounding alarmed.

"I am *so* sick. I can't get up, I can't take care of her, I can't walk the dog, I can't do anything."

"What do you want to do? Do you want to go to the doctor?"

"I DON'T KNOW! I don't *know* what to do — I don't get sick! I never get sick! And it's Sunday, and nobody's open…"

"I'm coming over."

When Allen gets here, I'm still on the couch. I haven't moved an inch, in fact. I'm just sitting there on the couch in a daze.

"What do you want to do?" he asks me again.

"Allen, I don't know, I don't know, I can't even decide if I need to pee or not."

Did I take something? Some medicine? No. Well, um, yes, this morning I guess. Tylenol, or something. How about taking something now?

"Dammit, Allen, I can't stand taking medicine!"

"How do you expect to feel any better if you don't take anything for it? Just take something, and you can worry about not liking to take anything later."

I struggle to drag myself off of the couch and down the hall to the bathroom. Okay, okay. A couple of more Tylenol. When I sit back down on the couch, I voice to him what has been going through my mind, but I haven't had the guts to say it yet.

"Allen, I can't do this."

"Do what?"

"Katherine. I can't do this. I can't take care of her, I can't be there for her, I can't give her what she needs, I can't even figure out what that is right now! I can't be a mom, I can hardly *lift* her I'm so weak, and she only weighs fifteen pounds! I can't think, I can't even smile for her. She thinks I hate her."

"No she doesn't and yes, Ellen, you can do this. You did do this. You were her mom, and you are her mom. You just have to take care of yourself and get better."

"The last time I was sick like this was years ago, and it took me *months* to get better. Months! That wasn't just physically, that was mentally, too! And that was when I didn't have anyone else to take care of. She's going to be scarred for *life* by then; I'll have given her serious psychological problems, and she'll spend her whole life in therapy, and she's better off without me than with me if I'm screwing her up."

Allen has never seen me like this. Actually, no one has ever seen me like this. The only Ellen my friends have ever known is the 'always have it together and have everything under control' Ellen. Now, I'm a nutcase. A crying, shaking nutcase.

"How much sleep have you been getting?" he asks me.

"Not much, she tosses and turns at night, and wakes up and cries, and I'm such a light sleeper…"

"She's sleeping in your room??" he says in disbelief.

"Well…yeah. She was so used to being in my room with me, that I didn't want to throw that in on her as well. She's had a hard enough transition as it is. So her crib is by my bed."

After a moment, Allen says, "Sleep at my place tonight. I'll sleep here."

"You can't do that…"

"I can. Let's go over to my place, you stay there, and I'll go get Katherine from your friend's and bring her back here. Go get your stuff together."

"Allen, you're too busy to be doing this…thank you…"

I get my things together, and we head over to his apartment, which is barely a half-mile away. This is where our meditation group meets, in his living room. I go and lie down on the Victorian sofa in the living room while he changes the sheets on his bed. It is still and intense and peaceful in here. There are ten years' worth of meditation vibes humming off of the walls. Allen comes in and lays a quilt over me, then leaves to finish straightening his room.

"Thank you, Allen," I say again, and start to tear up. "I never thought that I would be one of your causes."

"No problem."

That night, I sit up in bed and practice my breathing. I am savoring every moment of the quiet stillness in Allen's apartment. Breathing in, I feel at peace. Breathing out, I feel at peace. Right now, at this moment, those are just words. I do not feel at peace. I do not feel relaxed and all right. But the Tylenol have kicked in, so my head and face are down to a dull pounding. I may not feel at peace, but the quiet is starting to seep into my consciousness. And that's a start.

July 3rd

KATHERINE AND I SPEND THE DAY doing mommy-daughter things. Having a latte and scone outside of Elliot's, our local coffeehouse. A leisurely start to the day, to be followed by a trip to the beach. Sushi for dinner. The guy who makes the sushi is from Vietnam; he came over at 16 in the eighties from a refugee camp and lived with a family in Chesapeake, Virginia. Katherine is his favorite customer. He mixes her up a bowl of rice and roe, and slides me extra sushi and rolls to try on the sly. We like him back! She has a little trouble prying the sticky sushi rice out of the bowl with her spoon, but heaven forbid I reach over to help her. I know from experience that this would elicit flinging both bowl and spoon to the floor.

I turn 39 today. It is almost half a year since we returned from Vietnam. It's been a step-by-step journey, creating this new life of ours. A huge dose of antibiotics finally got me on the road to recovery. And we found new daycare, ten blocks away from where I live with a woman, Joanne, who is a stay-at-home mom with her own two kids. The first full week, Katherine was a miserable, inconsolable little girl. It is amazing that she had any vocal chords left. On the fourth day, Joanne tells me that she had left some colored bowls scattered on the floor, and a little while later had turned to see them all neatly stacked. No one was near, other than a glum little Katherine moping a few feet away. Joanne spread the bowls out again and Katherine sat unmoving. Twenty minutes later, the bowls were again neatly stacked. There was no confession out of Katherine.

Then, on Friday afternoon, the fifth day, a popcorn fight broke out in the kitchen amongst the other children. Katherine sat there stunned at first, then broke into squeals of laughter. With that, the walls came tumbling down.

A month later, just before Easter, she took her second 'first' steps. And we finally had a chance to go to New Jersey to visit family and stay with grandma and also Auntie Susan. She figured out which star on the wall concealed the peek-a-boo fairy, she conducts to her toy piano, she feeds Milkbones to the dog, and is very enthusiastic when she waves bye-bye.

A year has passed since I sat in this very spot the day that I turned 38. That day I contemplated the lack of Mr. Right in my life and my desire for a family. Of how this lack of a nurturing, sharing partnership was obstructing my wish to become a mother, and there didn't seem to be anything that I could do about that. I wanted smiles and snuggles and giggles, crayon pictures on the refrigerator, someone to bake and decorate cookies with at Christmas-time, and little socks to match up when I was doing laundry. I was angry and sad and frustrated that somehow this basic, fundamental need seemed to have eluded me.

I searched my mind for options that day. Two years before that, a family friend, a single woman, adopted a little girl from China.

Could I see myself doing that? Could I make such a thing manifest in my life? That day was the day my journey began.

MY LIFE HAS CHANGED in many of the ways that I had expected, and then some. I can no longer spontaneously head down to the local arts cinema to catch a foreign film at night. Ditto calling friends for a short-notice bite to eat. My priority list for cleaning the house, doing the dishes and laundry, and getting office work done on the computer has gotten a little more flexible. *Everything* revolves around Katherine-time. When she'll be up, when she'll be eating, when she'll be napping, when she'll be at daycare, when I'll be picking her up, when she'll be going to bed. My non-Katherine life gets squeezed-in around those moments. I am always on alert. Watching for things that can hurt her, watching for things to amuse her. Or just watching her.

One thing that I didn't expect: my short-term memory is in the trashcan (probably next to the sippy-cups that she likes to drop in there). I have come up with the theory that there is a limit to the amount of multi-tasking that a brain can handle at once. Kinda like when you try to run too many programs at once on your computer. It crashes. I compensate for this first by accepting this fact, and second, by making little notes about every little thing and pasting them all over the house. On the fridge, bathroom mirror, the back of the front door, on the steering wheel of the car.

But my Katherine-life! She is an angel. She is magnetic. She is ecstatic. She is joyous. She is funny. She is open and charming and gregarious, and total strangers can't help but smile when we pass them on the street or sit while I have my latte. I have all those things that I wanted and more. This life that we have together is so fulfilling...so *full*. So much so that if a partner doesn't come along, it will be OK. Selfishly, I'm sometimes not so sure that I *want* to share her with anyone.

My goal when we are together is to make Katherine-time be Katherine's time. She has all of me then. I'm not trying to do something else during this time (all that does is piss her off, and I end up not getting it done anyway), and I'm trying not to worry about tedious things. At least, that's my goal. I don't always succeed. This is my mommy-mindfulness. My Buddhist Practice. As it turns out, this doesn't just benefit her: it is a gift to me. I watch and am a part of her little first-time enlightenments. As sand trickles through her fingers. Or as she rides on a carousel. Or sees a real live horse.

She is still *une petite jeune fille* at under twenty pounds. She says "da-da" for doggie, "na-na" for banana, "Hi!" "Bye!" "Thank you!" and "chicken." Chicken is a weird one. She knows that it means a chicken, but she also knows that it's something on her plate. I can tell that she wonders about this, and I'm sure she'll be horrified the day she finds out why this is so. Maybe that day we'll go back to being vegetarian!

She has learned in the past few weeks that she can initiate hugs and kisses instead of only participating in them. She has put this new discovery into fervent practice, and it melts me in a way that nothing ever has. It is effortless to meet one of my daily goals: to lose track of how many times I say "I love you" to her. She loves music and dancing and Indian food and swinging at the playground. I get to give myself the excuse that when we are together, there is nothing else more important that I need to be doing. License to goof off and just have fun. To open my eyes and see the world through hers. Do the dishes sit in the sink for a couple of days at a time? Sometimes. Have I opened my bank statements since Spring? Nope. Does it bother me? Nope.

November 11th

TODAY KATHERINE TURNS TWO. To celebrate, we go to an Italian restaurant with three of my girlfriends…no other kids, so she is the special little princess tonight. Katherine is entranced by the singing waiters and plays with ice cubes. Then, after the meal, she finally gets the idea of presents and wrapping paper. She tears at the colorful paper with gusto, shrieking with excitement at each discovered treasure inside.

The next holiday that I look forward to is not Christmas or Hanukah, although we get to do both because of two sides of the family (Buddhist license for flexibility). It is December 12th, the day that Katherine was placed in my arms. Actually, the day that she lifted her arms up to me to say "I'm yours!" In adoption-speak, this is called our "gotcha day." It is a different kind of birthday for us. It is the day that our little family of two was born. I'm not sure what yet, but we are going to do something special.

Last week she graduated from calling me 'mama' to 'mom-meeee!' She says 'no' to anything that sounds like a question. She has also grasped the concept of "Mine!" No matter what her mood, she is only moments away from a fit of giggles, and mommy knows just how to get them out of her. She can give high-fives and low-fives, and is fascinated with babies whenever and wherever she sees one. She would make such a great big sister, I think. Which, of course, brings on the thought of how that could someday happen. If I did meet someone, would I like to have, to give birth to, a child? I think so. If that didn't happen though, I would hop online in an instant. "Binh? Are you too busy to take another one on again?" The cost for Katherine's adoption, including travel and living there for two months, ended up being around $13,000. I would do it again in a heartbeat. If I couldn't have a biological child, I can honestly say that I would not have a single moment's regret, a feeling of missing something if it were just the two of us. Talk about taking the biological-clock pressure off!

WHEN PEOPLE SEE US, they often remark at how lucky this little girl is, and what a wonderful thing it is that I have done. On the contrary. It is I who feel lucky…and blessed. She has been a gift to me, and I am thankful each day beyond measure.

The other day, I opened up my Vietnam journal, just to relive some of our adventure. I have done this several times over the past half year, but I saw something that had slipped by me the last times. This time, I read about the dream that I had had that first night at the Army Guesthouse. A dream that I had completely forgotten about. Where I kept forgetting my daughter, *Lily*, everywhere I went, and then leaving her and hearing very distinctly "You are not my mother." That little girl in my dream with the solemn face was right. I was not her mother. Another child…*this* child…was waiting for me.

I HAVEN'T HAD AS MUCH TIME to sit and meditate these days, so I'm not any better at it. Even our visits to meditation group are once a month now, and we just stay for the first twenty-or-so minutes during sharing time until Katherine gets restless. A toddler in the room is not conducive to silent contemplation. But everyone loves to see her and watch her grow. They feel like part of her spiritual family, and know about everything that I went through to bring her into my life.

Do I have any regrets? Not about her. Sometimes I see families, a mommy and a daddy and a little one, and when the child does something funny or cute, mommy and daddy get to share a glance with each other, they get to share that wonderful experience. It used to give me a twinge that when I look up there is no one else to look back. I don't look up anymore. It is Katherine's and my shared moment.

She brings such joy into my life that some nights I still wander into her room to watch her sleep to remind myself that she really is here. When I hear her soft, rhythmic breathing, I can't help but synchronize my own breath with my daughter's, and it becomes a meditation. Breathing in, I feel calm, I feel at peace. Breathing out, I feel calm, I feel at peace.

She is my Katherine, my daughter, who is everything that I had hoped she would be and more. She is her own great presence, and sometimes I still feel like simply a caretaker and guide for this being who chose to be with me for this time around. Perhaps she knows something that I don't. She has enriched my life, and expanded my heart. As for my old life, yes, I've given things up, but I'm still me. Only now it's 'we,' and it's 'our' life. It's our *destiny*, our *duyen phan*.

Chapter opening photograph: Forbidden City, Hue, Vietnam

十二

Afterword

ADOPTING KATHERINE not only opened up the world of motherhood to me, but many other worlds as well. The moment "American" became a part of Katherine's identity, my identity changed with it. I became a mommy. I became a part of an Asian-American family. I became not just a parent, but an adoptive parent. And, because my child is not Caucasian, we are a billboard every moment that we are out in public. Which makes me a sometimes willing, sometimes not so, adoption advocate.

People can't help but to make assumptions when they see us, as people tend to do when anyone is different:

That's one of those Chinese babies.

She must have been infertile…

I hear the conditions in those orphanages are terrible…

Is she 'bonding' well?

Was she abandoned?

Why didn't you adopt a waiting American child?

Don't 'those people' know about birth control?

How could a mother ever give up her child?

Where is her 'real' mother?

What a lucky little girl, she'll have a much better life here…

All of these statements or questions have either been spoken to me or I have heard them whispered nearby. Sometimes I have the energy for an answer, sometimes I don't…sometimes I'm too polite to say what I really want to:

No she's not, she's from Vietnam.

No, I'm not, and it's none of your business.

Sometimes yes, sometimes no…it's a shame that due to unfortunate circumstances there are children in the world who don't have a loving family who can afford to feed them. What are YOU doing to help?

(Drop-jawed shock that someone asked that to our faces after watching Katherine and I in joyous exchange)

Ditto.

Many are special needs or older or with emotional issues from bouncing around in the foster care system. I'm a single mom and know what I'm capable of handling right now. How many of them have you adopted?

In third-world countries, there isn't always the information and resources to ensure dependable birth control. And abortion is not an option when a pregnant mother knows that she will be unable to care for a child.

It is the hardest thing in the world.

I'm her 'real' mother.

I'm the lucky one.

And so I am. Enlightened people just tell me "What a beautiful little girl!" (She is). Occasionally I meet an older Caucasian man, woman or couple, and their faces light up to see her…I know what they're going to tell me: "We have an Asian granddaughter, and she's the light of our lives!" They know. They know. We have been blessed with gifts from afar.

Along with my regular duties as a parent, my job as Katherine's mommy will grow to include being a support for her sense of self as she realizes that she's different. She's adopted. She's a member of a minority. People will make certain assumptions about her based on how she looks. Bigots will say certain things to her for the same reason. She will sometimes be treated differently—perhaps badly—because of the color of her skin. May I have the patience, the sensitivity, the awareness and the compassion to help her, help us, through these difficult issues. In the U.S., over 20,000 children were adopted internationally in 2002. Our children come from Russia, China, Korea, Guatemala, Vietnam and Cambodia, just to name a few of countries. Our multi-cultural families are changing the face of American families! I wish the day comes soon when ALL of the people living in the world around us can see and embrace the richness there is to be found in diversity.

A woman far away across the world once made a decision, a selfless decision that caused her great pain. It sorrows me that she had that decision to make. In a twist of fate, her circumstance has brought great joy into my life. I think about that often. And I trust that someday in the greater scheme of things, sorrow, joy, fairness, love and destiny will all make sense.

Etiquette for the non-adoptive person

To start off with, please be mindful of what you say in front of a child. They hear and understand more than you know. Don't risk causing emotional trauma just to satisfy your curiosity.

Biological parent, or birthmother/birthfather. The mother and father who physically are responsible for the birth of this child. Not 'real,' not 'natural.' An adoptive parent is just as real and natural as any other parent.

Abandoned, orphanage. There are many reasons why a child is available for adoption. People are familiar with China's much-publicized one-child-only policy, and that little girls are relinquished for adoption in favor of little boys. There might be the social stigma of an unwed mother. Or perhaps the child was born into such poverty that the mother or parents are unable to care for them. Regardless of the situation, if you are a complete stranger to an adoptive parent that you run into, it is less than polite to press for such details of their family matters.

Cost. Yes, the cost of the adoptive process can unfortunately run into tens of thousands of dollars. We did not 'pay' for the child, we paid for the tedious process of documentation and lawyers and translators and orphanage donations and agency fees.

Bonding and adjusting. Children are such amazingly resilient beings, and I was totally amazed at my own daughter's "go with the flow" attitude from day one. Most children do stunningly well. And for those that do have difficulties, it's really a private matter. If you see a parent and child obviously enamored of each other, what else is there to say?

Support. A family that came to be through adoption is just as much a 'real' family as any other. A mother waiting to bring home a son or daughter is just as deserving of a baby shower as a pregnant mother. The arrival of a child just as deserving of a celebration. Educate yourself, educate those around you. Be respectful, be considerate.

FJK

Resources

ADOPTION RESOURCES

These sites were chosen for their comprehensive nature. Most of them have their own extensive links and resources lists.

Independent Adoption Network: Information regarding independent international adoption for various countries. *www.IndependentAdoptionNetwork.org*.

International Adoption News: Up-to-date news and information from and about the international adoption community. *www.InternationalAdoptionNews.com*.

Adoptive Parents of Vietnam: Newsgroup that supports people interested in, in the process of, or post-adoptive, from Vietnam. *http://groups-beta.google.com/group/apv/*.

Comeunity: Information on adoption from Vietnam and elsewhere. *http://www.comeunity.com*

Families with Children from Vietnam: Support and information for families with children adopted from Vietnam. *http://www.fcvn.org/*

NAIC: National Adoption Information Clearinghouse — a comprehensive resource on all aspects of adoption. Operated by the U.S. Department of Health and Human Services. Resources for adoption professionals, adopted persons, birthparents, prospective and adoptive parents, adoption-oriented publications, agency information, adoption statistics, and access to thousands of research documents, as well as an extensive listing of adoption-related conferences held nationwide. *http://naic.acf.hhs.gov/*

Joint Council on International Children's Services: an affiliation of licensed, non-profit international adoption organizations from around the world. *http://www.jcics.org/*

U.S. State Department: The US State Department's policies on International adoptions. General information and country-by-country listing of adoption requirements. *http://travel.state.gov/adopt.html*

Evan B. Donaldson Adoption Institute: a national not-for-profit organization devoted to improving adoption policy and practice. *http://www.adoptioninstitute.org/*

The Center for Adoption Support and Education, Inc. (C.A.S.E.): provides post-adoption counseling and educational services to families, educators, child welfare staff, and mental health providers in Maryland, Northern Virginia, and Washington, D.C. In addition, C.A.S.E. is a national resource for families and professionals through its training, publications, and consultations. Has an extensive links page to other adoption resources. *http://www.adoptionsupport.org/*

American Adoption Congress: The American Adoption Congress is composed of individuals, families and organizations committed to adoption reform. http://www.americanadoptioncongress.org/

Dave Thomas Foundation for Adoption: increasing the awareness and adoption of the more than 150,000 children in North America's foster care system. *http://www.davethomasfoundationforadoption.org/*

Lets Talk Adoption: website for a weekly adoption-oriented radio show. Listen live, or to streaming audio of archived shows. Archives include interviews with adoption professionals, attorneys, researchers, organization and foundation leaders. *http://www.letstalkadoption.com/*

Inter-National Adoption Alliance: a national adoption education and advocacy organization joining domestic and international adoptees and their families. *http://www.i-a-a.org/home.htm*

OTHER RESOURCES

Recommended reading (personal favorites):

Peace is Every Step, by Thich Nhat Hanh
The Miracle of Mindfulness, by Thich Nhat Hanh
After the Ecstasy, the Laundry, by Jack Kornfield
Wherever You Go, There You Are: Mindfulness Meditation in Everyday Life, by Jon Kabat-Zinn

Lovingkindness: The Revolutionary Art of Happiness, by Sharon Salzberg

Each Breath a Smile (for children), by Thich Nhat Hanh

Recommended surfing

For more about the social projects in Vietnam of the Mindfulness Community of Hampton Roads, visit: *www.MindfulnesscommunityofHR.com*

To find out more about the teachings and work of Thich Nhat Hanh, visit *www.plumvillage.org*

Books by Thich Nhat Hanh, for children and adults, are available at your bookstore, or visit *www.parallax.org*.

FJK

About the Author

DR. ELLEN FITZENRIDER has her undergraduate degree in English from Rutgers University in 1985 and her Doctor of Chiropractic in 1991. Her travels have taken her from Maine to California to the Caribbean, from the Scottish Highlands to Morocco, and now Southeast Asia. She has been a practitioner of Vietnamese Buddhism for nine years. She currently lives, works, is a mommy and tries to be mindful, in Norfolk, Virginia.

Lang Son, Katherine's Birthplace

Title and body set in Hiroshige 10.5 | 14.5

Based on woodblock prints by the famous Japanese artist,
Hiroshige Ando, Hiroshige was designed by Cynthia
Hollandsworth in 1986 for AlphaOmega Typography, Inc. Its
calligraphic feel makes it an excellent companion for Ex Ponto.

Chapter titles set in Ex Ponto

Ex Ponto was designed by acclaimed calligrapher,
type designer and artist Jovica Veljovic. Based on Veljovic's
handwriting, Ex Ponto's natural feel in combination with
careful craftsmanship make it a superb script typeface.